Asia's Latent Nuclear Powers:
Japan, South Korea and Taiwan

Mark Fitzpatrick

 **IISS** The International Institute for Strategic Studies

The International Institute for Strategic Studies

Arundel House | 13–15 Arundel Street | Temple Place | London | WC2R 3DX | UK

First published February 2016 **Routledge**
4 Park Square, Milton Park, Abingdon, Oxon, OX14 4RN

for **The International Institute for Strategic Studies**
Arundel House, 13–15 Arundel Street, Temple Place, London, WC2R 3DX, UK
www.iiss.org

Simultaneously published in the USA and Canada by **Routledge**
270 Madison Ave., New York, NY 10016

Routledge is an imprint of Taylor & Francis, an Informa Business

DIRECTOR-GENERAL AND CHIEF EXECUTIVE Dr John Chipman
EDITOR Dr Nicholas Redman
EDITORIAL MANAGER Nancy Turner
EDITORIAL Anna Ashton, Bonnie Bley, Jill Lally, Chris Raggett
COVER/PRODUCTION John Buck, Kelly Verity

The International Institute for Strategic Studies is an independent centre for research, information and debate on the problems of conflict, however caused, that have, or potentially have, an important military content. The Council and Staff of the Institute are international and its membership is drawn from almost 100 countries. The Institute is independent and it alone decides what activities to conduct. It owes no allegiance to any government, any group of governments or any political or other organisation. The IISS stresses rigorous research with a forward-looking policy orientation and places particular emphasis on bringing new perspectives to the strategic debate.

The Institute's publications are designed to meet the needs of a wider audience than its own membership and are available on subscription, by mail order and in good bookshops. Further details at www.iiss.org.

Printed and bound in Great Britain by Bell & Bain Ltd, Thornliebank, Glasgow

British Library Cataloguing in Publication Data
A catalogue record for this book is available from the British Library

Library of Congress Cataloging in Publication Data

ADELPHI series
ISSN 1944-5571

ADELPHI 455
ISBN 978-1-138-93080-3

Asia's Latent Nuclear Powers:
Japan, South Korea and Taiwan

Mark Fitzpatrick

Contents

ACKNOWLEDGEMENTS

The author is indebted to Fred McGoldrick, David Santoro, Joshua Pol-
lack, Alan Romberg, James Acton, Takaaki Daitoku, William Choong, Dr
Paul Irwin Crookes and Nobuyasu Abe for their helpful suggestions in
reviewing portions of this book. They and many others also gave freely
of their time in often lengthy interviews. Interviewees included Haruyuki
Aikawa, Dr Nobumasa Akiyama, David Albright, Ambassador Cho
Chang-beom, Ambassador Chun Yungwoo, Toby Dalton, Robert Einhorn,
Ambassador Tetsuya Endo, Dr Shu Yuan Hsieh, Dr Yoichi Funabashi, Dr
Katsuhisa Furukawa, Dr Michael Green, Dr Hahm Chaibong, Takuya Hat-
tori, Corey Hinderstein, Dr Hong Kyudok, Dr Richard Juichou Hu, Dr Jo
Dong-joon, Dr Jun Bong-geun, Dr Kim Changsu, Dr Kim Jiyoon, Dr Kim
Taewoo, Dr Lee Sang Hyun, Dr Liu Fu-kuo, Yosuke Naoi, Masakatsu Ota,
Dr Douglas Paal, Dr James Przystup, Dr Ely Ratner, Ambassador Yukio
Satoh, Dr James Schoff, Leonard (Sandy) Spector, Dr Tatsujiro Suzuki,
Sugio Takahashi, Dr Wang Yu-lung, Dr Tsuneo Watanabe, Chris Wood, Dr
Andrew Yang, David Yao, Dr Yim Man-sung, Youn Jong Kwon and anony-
mous officials in four capitals. Alireza Shams Lahijani provided research
assistance.

The Japan Institute for International Affairs, the Japanese National Institute for Defense Studies and the Center for Security Studies at National
Chengchi University held round-table discussions on my behalf that
brought insights and clarity to the issues, as did a conference hosted by
the Nuclear Nonproliferation Education and Research Center at the Korea
Atomic Energy Research Institute. Taiwan's Institute of Nuclear Energy
Research provided a detailed briefing, as did several other institutes and
government bodies in Taiwan during a tour by UK-based academics
organised by the Taiwan Ministry of Foreign Affairs that the author had
the good fortune to lead.

Finally, the author appreciates the unconditional support he received
from his wife, Kyoko, while working on the manuscript. This book is dedicated to their sons, Thomas and Robert, whose births in Seoul and Tokyo
respectively underscore the author's personal attachment to the region.

GLOSSARY

A2AD	anti-access/area-denial
AIT	American Institute in Taiwan
AEC	Atomic Energy Council (Taiwan)
AVLIS	atomic vapour laser isotope separation (an enrichment method)
CIA	Central Intelligence Agency
CEP	circular error probable
CSIST	Chung-Shan Institute of Science and Technology (Taiwan)
CTBT	Comprehensive Nuclear-Test-Ban Treaty
DPJ	Democratic Party of Japan
DPP	Democratic Progressive Party (Taiwan)
DPRK	Democratic People's Republic of Korea
EDD	Extended Deterrence Dialogue (Japan–US)
Euratom	European Atomic Energy Community
FBR	fast-breeder reactor
FCA	Fast Critical Assembly
HEU	highly enriched uranium
IAEA	International Atomic Energy Agency
ICBM	intercontinental ballistic missile
INER	Institute for Nuclear Energy Research (Taiwan)
JDA	Japan Defense Agency
JSDF	Japan Self-Defense Forces
KAERI	Korea Atomic Energy Research Institute
KMT	Kuomintang (Taiwan)

LDP	Liberal Democratic Party (Japan)
LEU	low-enriched uranium
MOX	mixed-oxide
MWt	Megawatt thermal
NPP	nuclear power plant
NPR	Nuclear Posture Review (US)
NPT	Non-Proliferation Treaty
NTD	New Taiwan Dollar
PRC	People's Republic of China
PSI	Proliferation Security Initiative
ROC	Republic of China
ROK	Republic of Korea
SLV	space-launch vehicle
SWU	separative work unit
THAAD	Terminal High Altitude Area Defense
TLAM-N	*Tomahawk* Land Attack Missile (nuclear-armed)
TRA	Taiwan Relations Act

The three Northeast Asian democracies that are the focus of this book are not suspected of nuclear proliferation. Japan, the Republic of Korea (ROK, or South Korea) and Taiwan (the Republic of China) have accepted all relevant global non-proliferation instruments and are in good standing with their obligations. They promote non-proliferation abroad, and their open, free societies would not sustain secret nuclear programmes at home. Yet each of the three makes for an interesting case study on potential proliferation. Ample grounds for analysis are provided by their advanced industries for nuclear and other dual-use technologies, their past pursuit of nuclear weapons and their desire to avert threats posed by nuclear-armed adversaries.

Global attention to the danger of nuclear proliferation is generally focused on the states that lie outside the Nuclear Non-Proliferation Treaty (NPT) or that have violated key requirements of the treaty. North Korea, Iran, Pakistan, Syria and, until recently, Iraq, Libya and Myanmar have been the usual suspects. India and Israel are also among the outliers. One reason for concern is that nuclear proliferation often has a knock-on effect. Acquisition of the atomic bomb by the United States, which had pooled knowledge with the United Kingdom, spurred the Soviet Union to keep pace. The Soviets then shared A-bomb technology with China, which led India to seek a nuclear equaliser. With help from China, Pakistan matched India. Due to these and other cases, the domino theory became a staple of the nuclear-proliferation literature.

It has often been presumed that Iran's development of sensitive nuclear technology could spur Saudi Arabia and perhaps other neighbours to do the same. In assessing the prospects for nuclear dominoes in the Middle East, it is useful to observe the situation in Northeast Asia, a region that recently saw the emergence of a new nuclear-armed state. At the beginning of this century, many observers predicted that if North Korea acquired nuclear weapons, it would be a game changer that could very likely cause Japan, South Korea and probably Taiwan to also do so. By 2016, Northeast Asia could have six nuclear-armed states, warned one American scholar.[1] Yet North Korea's nuclear test in 2006 and those that followed did not cause any of its neighbours to follow suit. Nor did China's 1964 test spark nuclearisation elsewhere (although not for lack of trying, in Taiwan's case). One purpose of this *Adelphi* book is to examine why this is, and to ask whether the current situation will hold.

The Iran nuclear issue provides another reason for writing this book. Iran has frequently insisted that, with regard to its nuclear programme, it simply wishes to be treated in the same manner as Japan: to be allowed a uranium-enrichment programme for civilian purposes, in accordance with the NPT. This claim has been met with incredulity by most Western experts. Iran's nuclear-safeguards violations, inadequate transparency and development work related to nuclear weapons stand in sharp contrast to Japan's clean record. This disparity may now change. Iran's acceptance in July 2015 of extensive verification measures under the accord negotiated in Vienna known as the Joint Comprehensive Plan of Action brings its status closer to that of Japan. The uranium-enrichment programme allowed for under the agreement, especially when limits on centrifuge numbers and type expire in 15 years, also brings Iran closer to its goal of Japan-equivalent treatment – to the dismay of critics. The expansion of sensitive fuel-cycle technologies – uranium enrichment[2] and plutonium reprocessing[3] – is perhaps the greatest proliferation concern today. As two American nuclear-policy scholars recently put it, 'nuclear latency is the new nuclear proliferation'.[4]

Many South Koreans have also lobbied for their country to be allowed these technologies. Enrichment and reprocessing have legitimate civilian purposes, but they also provide two paths to a nuclear weapon, and thus have been subjected to attempts at restriction by the US. In the post-war period, the authoritarian governments of South Korea and Taiwan pursued these technologies for non-peaceful purposes, before they were stopped by Washington. During the Second World War, Japan also sought nuclear weapons via both paths.

Circumstances are different today. It would be unprecedented for a US security partner to break its non-proliferation obligations. Only if circumstances dramatically changed in ways that simultaneously enlarged threat perceptions and diminished the credibility of the US security link would indigenous nuclearisation become a consideration for any of these three actors. Yet a nuclear-hedging option is another matter.

Given the well-developed status of their civilian nuclear industries, all three democracies in Northeast Asia can be called latent nuclear powers.[5] They could produce nuclear weapons without outside help within a few years or less, but they choose to refrain from doing so. Nuclear latency is most pronounced in Japan, due to its reprocessing and enrichment capabilities. Japan is often said also to employ a nuclear-hedging strategy, which analysts Wyn Bowen and Matthew Moran pithily define as 'nuclear latency with intent'.[6] South Korea and Taiwan have also at times considered nuclear hedging and it would not take long for them to acquire these technologies if they chose to break away from US-imposed restrictions. The main chapters in this book examine the state of nuclear technology in each of the three states, and assess how long it might take them to produce nuclear weapons, if the fateful decision to do so was taken.

The potential timeline for nuclearisation is another staple of the proliferation literature. In 2010 political scientist Scott Sagan provided the best summary of the literature, according to which the timeline is between four years and less than one year for countries that have access to fissile material, such as Japan, and longer for those without plutonium or enriched uranium.[7] Nonetheless, the assessments are often mechanistic, based on engineering formulas divorced from real-world context. Estimates vary widely depending on assumptions about the corners a state might be willing to cut and the nature of the arsenal it desires. If in an extremely dire situation a state decided it needed nuclear weapons as quickly as possible, its leaders might sideline issues of nuclear safety, warhead reliability, political and diplomatic considerations, and legal niceties. A more careful developmental process, as pursued by nearly every nuclear-armed state to date, could multiply the length of the timeline manyfold. Producing a handful of bombs at breakneck speed might not be the path taken by a nation that sought a survivable and robust nuclear deterrent.

Any decision to go nuclear would be affected foremost by the nature of the perceived threat. For Japan and Taiwan, this means the threat from China, in terms of both its nuclear and conventional capabilities. For South Korea (and to some degree Japan) North Korea's nuclear threat, exacerbated by its 6 January claimed hydrogen-bomb test, is a dominant factor. Other motivations are possible in the future. Japan worries, for example, about the prospect of an antagonistic unified Korea that has inherited nuclear-weapons technology from the North. South (and North) Koreans have their own concerns about Japan.

Such concerns increase the likelihood of a nuclear cascade. Japan's acquisition of nuclear weapons would give South Korea an almost irresistible motivation to follow suit. The same may also hold true for the reverse case, although this is less certain, given Japan's stronger societal aversion to nuclear weapons. The breakdown in the global non-proliferation order that would ensue from either or both Japan and South Korea going nuclear could cause Taiwan to abandon its non-proliferation commitments as well. The nuclear domino theory that was seemingly taken as an article of faith among early theorists has been called into question by more recent studies.[8] Yet it is hard to put the nightmare scenario out of mind. South Korean President Park Geun-hye evoked it by commenting in May 2014 that a fourth North Korean nuclear test could topple nuclear dominoes in the region.[9]

The existence of a nuclear threat is not sufficient reason to go nuclear; if it were, all three states in question would have nuclear arms by now. In each case, the reliability of the US security commitment is the dominant variable. Maintaining the credibility of US extended deterrence is the strongest safeguard of nuclear non-proliferation in the region. This credibility is frequently questioned in Asian security circles, usually with positive conclusions. However, when US President Barack Obama failed to enforce his declared 'red line' on the Syrian government's use of chemical weapons against rebel forces, and when Russia occupied Crimea without a military response from the US and its NATO allies, questions were raised about how the US would respond to similar actions by China. The analogy is inapt, of course. Syrian rebels and Ukraine are not covered by US security commitments of any sort. But questions are still being asked about whether events in Crimea might embolden Beijing to take aggressive steps in places not covered by US extended deterrence, such as Vietnam's territorial waters and, arguably, Taiwan.[10]

This book does not predict that Beijing will be so blatantly aggressive, nor that the Northeast Asian democracies will seek nuclear armament. But it does assess the circumstances that could push them in this direction in the future. It also addresses what must be done to keep Asia's latent nuclear powers from moving up the hedging ladder. Reassuringly, most of the policies needed to prevent the nuclear dominoes from falling are already in place, although they require constant attention.

Notes

1 James Clay Moltz, 'Future Nuclear Proliferation Scenarios in Northeast Asia', *Nonproliferation Review*, vol. 13, no. 3, November 2006.

2 Uranium enrichment is the physical process of increasing the percentage of the fissile isotope U-235, which comprises 0.7% of uranium in the metal's natural state. Most nuclear-reactor fuel requires a concentrate of about 3.5% U-235, while weapons-grade uranium is around 90% enriched. In theory, nuclear weapons can be made with uranium enriched to only 20%, which is considered to be the cut-off point between low-enriched uranium and highly enriched uranium.

3 Plutonium reprocessing is the chemical process of separating the plutonium produced by irradiating uranium from other components of spent reactor fuel.

4 Jeffrey M. Kaplow and Rebecca Davis Gibbons, 'The Days after a Deal with Iran: Implications for the Nuclear Nonproliferation Regime', RAND Corporation, 2015, http://www.rand.org/content/dam/rand/pubs/perspectives/PE100/PE135/RAND_PE135.pdf.

5 Other oft-used terms include 'virtual', 'threshold' or 'recessed' nuclear capabilities, each of which connotes a robust level of development and ambiguous intent

that does not necessarily apply to all of the three cases.

6   Wyn Bowen and Matthew Moran, 'Iran's Nuclear Programme: A Case Study in Hedging?', *Contemporary Security Policy*, vol. 35, no. 1, April 2014. Other notable works on the subject include Stephen M. Meyer, *The Dynamics of Nuclear Proliferation* (Chicago, IL: University of Chicago Press, 1984); Ariel E. Levite, 'Never Say Never Again: Nuclear Reversal Revisited', *International Security*, vol. 27, no. 3, Winter 2002–03, pp. 59–88; and Scott D. Sagan, 'Nuclear Latency and Nuclear Proliferation', in William C. Potter and Gaukhar Mukhatzhanova (eds), *Forecasting Nuclear Proliferation in the 21ˢᵗ Century*, Volume 1: *The Role of Theory* (Stanford, CA: Stanford University Press, 2010).

7   Sagan, 'Nuclear Latency and Nuclear Proliferation'.

8   For early studies on the subject, see Lewis A. Dunn and Herman Kahn, *Trends in Nuclear Proliferation, 1975– 1995: Predictions, Problems, and Policy Options* (Washington, DC: Hudson Institute, 1976); and US Committee on Nuclear Proliferation, 'A Report to the President by the Committee on Nuclear Proliferation', 21 January 1965. For more recent studies, see Nicholas L. Miller, 'Nuclear Dominoes: A Self-Defeating Prophecy?' *Security Studies*, vol. 23, no. 1, 2014, pp. 33–73; and William Potter, 'Divining Nuclear Intentions: Review Essay', *International Security*, vol. 33, no. 1, Summer 2008.

9   Gerard Baker and Alastair Gale, 'South Korea President Warns on Nuclear Domino Effect', *Wall Street Journal*, 29 May 2014.

10   Nobumasa Akiyama, 'Japan's Disarmament Dilemma: Between the Moral Commitment and the Security Reality', in George P. Shultz and James E. Goodby (eds), *The War that Must Never Be Fought: Dilemmas of Nuclear Deterrence* (Stanford, CA: Hoover Institution Press, 2015), p. 466.

CHAPTER ONE

Republic of Korea

If a new nuclear-armed state were to emerge in Northeast Asia, it would most likely be the Republic of Korea (ROK). This observation is not meant to predict that South Korea will choose nuclear armament. Steadfast in its adherence to the Non-Proliferation Treaty (NPT), the government in Seoul firmly rejects the pro-nuclear arguments posed by a few politicians and commentators. Officials understand well the downsides that those advocates ignore: the damage that nuclearisation would cause to the nation's economy and international status due to direct and indirect sanctions, and the huge security risks in jeopardising its alliance with the US. Going nuclear would undermine US relations at the same time as it made South Korea more vulnerable. Yet these demerits are not readily apparent to the general public, two-thirds of whom voice support for nuclear weapons in polls.[1] Such polls suggest that the non-proliferation norm is still shallow in South Korea. Twice in the 1970s, the country pursued nuclear weapons – albeit under an authoritarian government. More recently, South Korean nuclear scientists transgressed International Atomic Energy Agency (IAEA) safeguards in conducting enrichment and reprocessing experiments. A nationalist desire to possess the rights to sensitive nuclear technology that Japan enjoys could eventually see South Korea moving purposefully towards a recessed weapons capability. Seoul is very unlikely to cross the nuclear-weapons threshold, however, as long as the US defence commitment remains credible.

Pursuit of nuclear weapons in the 1970s

For most of the 1970s, ROK president Park Chung-hee* oversaw a secret nuclear-weapons programme. The pursuit began in 1970, when Park established the Agency for Defense Development and the Weapons Exploitation Committee, responsible for weapons procurement and production under the tight control of the Blue House (as the president's executive office and residence is called, due to its distinctive blue-tiled roof). In late 1973, the committee, which included 20 scientists, completed a long-term plan for nuclear-weapons development that was expected to be executed within six to ten years.[2] The acquisition of plutonium-reprocessing technology became a top priority for the Korea Atomic Energy Research Institute (KAERI), which was already keen to develop the fuel cycle in connection with civilian nuclear power.

Park's weapons pursuit was born out of insecurity, particularly fear of being abandoned by the US. At the time, the Democratic People's Republic of Korea (DPRK, or North Korea) had a stronger economy and military, and an incessantly aggressive posture in regard to the South.[3] In January 1968, two incidents underscored the danger. On the 21st of the month, a North Korean commando team intent on assassinating Park came within 100m of the Blue House. Two days

---

* Per IISS practice, Korean names are written according to the Korean style of family name first, except for in citations of materials, in which they are listed according to the publication referenced.

later, North Korea seized the *USS Pueblo* – which had been monitoring electronic signals off the coast of Wonsan – and captured 82 members of its crew (who were subsequently held hostage for 11 months). In April 1969, North Korea shot down an American EC-121 reconnaissance plane in international airspace. Dissatisfaction with Washington's handling of these incidents contributed to Park's impression that the US lacked resolve in dealing with North Korean aggression.

His concern was exacerbated by president Richard Nixon's unexpected announcement, made in Guam on 25 July 1969, of a new policy of shifting the burden of Asian allies' conventional defence to the countries themselves.[4] Two years later, the US abruptly withdrew its Seventh Infantry Division from South Korea amid calls in Congress for additional withdrawals, despite Park's strong objections to the move. Nixon's rapprochement with China and downgrading of relations with the Republic of China (ROC, or Taiwan) in 1971–72 further undermined South Korean trust, especially given the parallels between the ROK and the ROC.[5] South Koreans worried that Washington might begin a dialogue with Pyongyang behind Seoul's back or accept Beijing's demand that all US troops be withdrawn from the Korean Peninsula.[6] Threat perceptions were magnified by the 1974 attempt to assassinate Park made by a Japanese-born North Korean (whose missed shot killed the president's wife); by the discovery of two infiltration tunnels, in 1974 and 1975; and by communist forces' takeover of South Vietnam, in 1975.

Concern about protecting the nation from an aggressive adversary amid doubts about the US commitment thus drove Park to look to nuclear weapons for protection. Officials secretly sought to purchase a heavy-water reactor from Canada; a spent-fuel reprocessing plant (suitable for separating 20kg of plutonium a year) from France;[7] and a mixed-oxide reprocessing laboratory from Belgium. These procurement efforts could not be hidden from US intelligence agencies, however, particularly as their vigilance had been heightened by India's 1974 nuclear test, which relied on plutonium from a Canadian-supplied reactor and heavy water originating in the US. Washington intervened with Ottawa, Paris and Brussels to prevent the sales, and threatened to block loans to South Korea's civilian nuclear-power programme. Secretary of state Henry Kissinger told Park the US would even end the alliance and withdraw its nuclear umbrella if the nuclear-weapons-development programme was not stopped.[8] Park had no choice but to acquiesce.

Yet even in 1968, before the weapons programme was initiated, South Korea had been hesitant to join the NPT. Worried about potential Chinese nuclear attacks and nuclear-weapons transfers to North Korea, Seoul did not want to limit its policy options. Only under pressure from the US and with the reassurance of Washington's security commitment did Seoul agree to sign the treaty that year, when it opened for signature,[9] although ratification only took place in 1975, after Park agreed to end the weapons programme.

Park's termination order was soon reversed. The November 1976 election of Jimmy Carter, who during the campaign had pledged to withdraw all US troops from South Korea and who had been highly critical of South Korean human-rights failings, confirmed Park's worst fears, prompting him to resume the secret nuclear programme. This time, however, he directed officials to seek technology indirectly, in a manner that would not invite foreign pressure. In December 1976, officials established the Korea Nuclear Fuel Development Institute, which sent researchers to France and Belgium to learn about reprocessing techniques. Work also began on designs for an indigenous plutonium-production reactor. US intelligence agencies learned of these efforts but could not find convincing evidence of weapons-related activity.

After Park was assassinated, in October 1979, his successor Chun Doo-hwan ended nuclear-weapons-related activities, disbanding a group of 870 scientists engaged in sensitive work.[10] Having seized power via a military coup and ruthlessly suppressed an uprising in Kwangju, Chun needed the legitimacy provided by friendly relations with the US.[11] By this time, Carter had scrapped his plans to withdraw troops and tactical nuclear weapons from South Korea. The Reagan administration, which came to power in 1981, provided a reinvigorated security guarantee while maintaining the threat of sanctions if activity related to nuclear weapons was not fully terminated, along with that for an associated missile-development programme.

Assessments vary on how close South Korea came to producing a nuclear weapon. A March 1975 State Department cable was sanguine in assessing that a limited weapons and missile capability could be developed in ten years. The US embassy in Seoul replied that South Korea's technical capabilities should not be underestimated, and that acquiring a nuclear weapon could take 'well less' than ten years.[12] Scientists involved in the programme told their superiors in 1978 that a weapon could be produced by 1981.[13] When nuclear engineers involved in the programme were later interviewed, however, they indicated that this claim was exaggerated; all the ROK had at the time were blueprints.[14] Indeed, South Korea had no reactor designed to produce weapons-grade plutonium,[15] no reprocessing plant or uranium-enrichment facility and no missiles capable of carrying nuclear warheads. The counter-factual claim that South Korea would have had nuclear weapons by the mid-1980s if the US had not intervened[16] is overstated.

South Koreans today have mixed views about the past pursuit of nuclear weapons. Even staunch non-proliferation advocates have defended Park on the grounds that he did what he thought was necessary to defend the nation. They also note that proliferation was the trend of the times, with 15 or more other countries possessing or seeking nuclear weapons.[17] One popular narrative is that Park was just bluffing in order to dissuade Washington from abandoning South Korea.

Looking back at Park's efforts and the inconsistent budgetary support for the programme, it appears that the purpose of at least the resumed 1977 programme was to create a weapons option, and not necessarily to produce weapons.[18] Blue House officials believed that the US would accept this capability in the ROK, just as it had Israel's presumptive nuclear-weapons programme.[19]

Although Chun extinguished the nuclear-weapons programme, questions occasionally arise as to whether the embers might still be glowing. In 1991, for example, it was reported that two years earlier, the Joint Chiefs of Staff had presented a proposal to defence minister Lee Sang-hoon for a full-scale resumption of the nuclear-weapons effort, under what was known as the 'Triple XXX Plan'. According to Suh Su-jong, who was then chief secretary to the director of the Agency for National Security Planning (formerly the Korea Central Intelligence Agency), president Roh Tae-woo did not definitively reject the Triple XXX Plan until mid-1991, when the US learned of it and forced him to dismiss scientists and engineers from suspected nuclear facilities near KAERI laboratories in Daejeon.[20]

Ambivalence about enrichment and reprocessing

On 8 November 1991, Roh issued a 'Declaration of Non-Nuclear Korean Peninsula Peace Initiatives', affirming that South Korea would not 'manufacture, possess, store, deploy or use nuclear weapons'. He also declared that South Korea 'will not possess nuclear fuel reprocessing and enrichment facilities'.[21] The no-storage element of the five nuclear 'noes' was the result of US president George H.W. Bush's announcement in September that year of the withdrawal of all ground-launched short-range nuclear weapons from foreign soil, and the removal of tactical nuclear weapons from surface ships, attack submarines and land-based naval aircraft. At the height of the Cold War, about 950 US nuclear weapons were stationed in South Korea.[22] Roh's statement remains a key element of South Korea's non-proliferation policy.

Roh's non-nuclear statement in turn paved the way for the 'Joint Declaration of South and North Korea on the Denuclearization of the Korean Peninsula', negotiated in late 1991 and signed in January 1992. The two sides agreed not to 'test, manufacture, produce, receive, possess, store, deploy or use nuclear weapons'. They also agreed not to 'possess nuclear reprocessing and uranium enrichment facilities'.[23] Verification measures that were to include reciprocal inspection visits were never implemented. Although North Korea has blatantly violated the agreement, forgoing enrichment and reprocessing remains the official policy of the ROK government.

Roh's forswearing of reprocessing and enrichment was largely the result of pressure from the US, which insisted that the disavowal not be time-limited, as the ROK had desired.[24] His willingness to forgo these sensitive nuclear technologies was controversial in the scientific and security communities, in which many argued that it unnecessarily restricted civilian nuclear technology and reduced diplomatic leverage vis-à-vis the North.[25]

Unsurprisingly, South Korea maintained an interest in developing the full fuel cycle. In 2004 information came to light about laboratory-scale experiments in uranium conversion, uranium enrichment and plutonium separation that took place at various times between 1982 and 2000. The experiments occurred in civilian settings; there were no indications of any military connection or that they were conducted according to a systematic plan.[26] The enrichment and reprocessing experiments were reported voluntarily, if belatedly, by the ROK in connection with its declaration to the IAEA pursuant to the Additional Protocol – the strengthened safeguards system that the agency introduced in 1997, in response to the discovery in the early 1990s of Iraq's hidden military nuclear programme.

Between 1993 and 2000, at least ten enrichment experiments involving exempted or undeclared nuclear material took place at KAERI facilities in Daejeon. These experiments used the atomic vapour laser isotope separation (AVLIS) method, producing a total of 200mg of enriched uranium, with an average enrichment level of about 10% U-235, and a maximum enrichment level of 77%. The ROK said that the experiments were authorised by no official higher than the president of KAERI, involved around 14 scientists and were conducted in the context of a stable isotope separation project (an effort not originally designed to enrich uranium). A previously unreported chemical-enrichment experiment was also carried out, between 1979 and 1981, producing a very small quantity of very slightly enriched uranium (0.72% U-235). While verifying the 2004 declaration, the IAEA learned that KAERI had also conducted unreported uranium-conversion work, producing about 154kg of natural (not enriched) uranium metal.[27]

The ROK also reported in 2004 that in 1982 a plutonium-separation experiment had been conducted at the TRIGA III research reactor in Seoul. The irradiation of 2.5kg of depleted uranium produced 0.7g of plutonium with an isotopic content of about 98% of Pu-239 – an extremely small amount of very high-grade material. The ROK said the experiment was conducted solely to satisfy the intellectual interests of the scientists involved.[28]

Although South Korea's failure to report the experiments earlier was clearly in contravention of its safeguards obligations,[29] the IAEA Board of Governors decided in November 2004 not to reach a finding of safeguards non-compliance, and therefore not to report the matter to the UN Security Council. In lieu of a board resolution, the chairman of the board issued a summary endorsing IAEA director general Mohamed ElBaradei's view that 'the failure of the Republic of Korea to report the activities in accordance with its safeguards agreements is of serious concern'.[30]

Political considerations were a major reason why there was no finding of non-compliance. The ROK and its supporters justified the board's lenient handling of the matter on the grounds that only small amounts of material were involved, and that Seoul had voluntary reported the experiments and thoroughly cooperated with the IAEA's verification activity. The South Koreans contended that by demonstrating the utility of the Additional Protocol they had strengthened the safeguards regime.[31] Insisting that it had only recently become aware of the experiments, the ROK intensively lobbied board members. The US did not want to embarrass its ally or give diplomatic ammunition to North Korea, which was under the spotlight for having announced its withdrawal from the NPT the year before. Another factor was that more egregious violations by Iran had not yet been reported to the Security Council.

In May 2008, four years after the reporting failures were identified, the IAEA concluded that it considered all of South Korea's past undeclared activities involving uranium enrichment and conversion, and plutonium separation, to have been resolved. The agency was also able to draw a 'broader conclusion' under the Additional Protocol that all nuclear material in the ROK was being used in peaceful activities.[32] Meanwhile, to promote transparency, the ROK revised its Atomic Energy Act and established the Korea Institute of Nuclear Nonproliferation and Control, which was entrusted with conducting national inspections.[33] None of the scientists involved in the experiments were punished, however. On the contrary, they are regarded as heroes by many fellow citizens for their efforts to strengthen Korea's energy security, and for resisting foreign-imposed restrictions on technological advancement.[34]

Capabilities

South Korea's robust nuclear-energy programme and industrial strength give it clear nuclear latency. With no oil and rapidly rising electricity demand, South Korea introduced nuclear power in the 1970s to address its paucity of indigenous energy sources. Today, its 24 nuclear-power reactors supply 29% of the nation's electricity. With another four reactors under construction and between four and eight more being planned, the country's nuclear-power capacity is expected to increase to about 32.9 gigawatts electrical, or nearly one-third of total national power supply, by 2022.[35] These expansion plans may be delayed by the growing anti-nuclear movement that took shape after the Fukushima disaster and that gained momentum after a series of nuclear-safety scandals erupted in 2013, but nuclear power has become central to the South Korean economy.

Lacking any significant proven uranium-ore deposits, South Korea imports uranium from Kazakhstan, Canada, Australia, Niger and elsewhere, and purchases enrichment services from France. Fuel for light- and heavy-water reactors is fabricated at facilities in Daejeon. Two early research reactors (Korea Research Reactors 1 and 2, which had capacities of 250 kilowatts and 2,000kw respectively) were phased out in 1995, and were replaced by the 30 megawatts thermal HANARO (High-flux Advanced Neutron Application Reactor), which is used for isotope production and research. A new 15MWt facility at Busan, the Kijang Research Reactor, is expected to begin operation in 2017.

In December 2009, South Korea became a nuclear-reactor exporter by winning a contract, worth US$20.4 billion, to supply four nuclear-power reactors to the United Arab Emirates (UAE). Four months later, South Korea contracted to provide a 5MWt research reactor to Jordan. Marketing its products in Lithuania, Romania, Turkey, Vietnam and elsewhere, the ROK seeks to capture 20% of the world market for nuclear reactors by 2030. In March 2015, KAERI signed an agreement with Saudi Arabia to assess the potential for building two or more newly developed 330MWt reactors named SMART (System-integrated Modular Advanced Reactor), which are ideal for seawater desalination.

South Korea is among the world's leaders in nuclear research and development. In particular, KAERI is working on new reactor designs and advanced nuclear fuel, as well as radioactive-waste management. Three different types of fast reactors are in development. In connection with the Generation IV International Forum, some of this work is being carried out in cooperation with the US Department of Energy. KAERI is evaluating methods of spent-fuel recycling, among other fuel-cycle technologies. South Korea is also one of seven members of the International Thermonuclear Experimental Reactor project, providing further evidence of its advanced status in nuclear technologies.

The ROK also has robust missile and aerospace programmes, and expertise in advanced solid-fuel technologies. The nation's conventional military capabilities include short-range ballistic and cruise missiles that are inherently capable of carrying nuclear weapons. Based on the US *Nike Hercules* ballistic missiles, South Korea's solid-fuelled *Hyunmu*-1 and -2 systems can carry payloads of 500kg. The missile has a diameter of 0.54m (which is smaller than most first-generation nuclear weapons). Their range was initially limited to 180km under US-imposed guidelines designed to demonstrate that they were not intended to carry nuclear weapons. That limit was extended to 300km in 2001, when South Korea joined the Missile Technology Control Regime, which restricts exported missiles with a 500kg warhead to this range (range and payload being interchangeable along a curve). In 2012 South Korea persuaded the US to allow a range up to 800km, which enables missiles fired from Daegu, in central South Korea, to reach all of North Korea. In the context of its new, proactive deterrence strategy, Seoul's request to extend the range was a response to North Korea's lethal provocations two years earlier (as discussed below).

Missiles of this range had already been in development before the range limit was extended, and are scheduled for deployment by 2017.[36] The range/payload interchangeability curve permits the ROK to develop ballistic missiles with a range of 400km and a payload of 1,000kg, allowing it to deliver a moderately advanced nuclear weapon anywhere in North Korea, if launched close to the border.[37] These ballistic missiles apparently incorporate advanced systems used in Russian intercontinental ballistic missiles (ICBMs).[38] South Korea's missile programme is more advanced than that of Japan, which has space-launch vehicles but no ground-launched missiles.

South Korea has also developed turbojet-propelled cruise missiles, which have a diameter of 0.52m and a payload capacity of 500kg, allowing them to be launched from destroyers and submarines. The latest version, the *Hyunmoo*-3C, has a maximum range of 1,500km and a circular error probable (CEP) of about 3m (meaning that one-half of the missiles launched against a specific target point will land within 3m of that point). Guidelines on unmanned aerial vehicles were relaxed in 2012 to allow payloads of 2,500kg (up from 500kg).

With technology assistance from Russia, South Korea's aerospace programme has developed a two-stage space-launch vehicle that successfully placed a satellite into orbit in 2013, after two failed attempts. A three-stage rocket designed to carry a 1.5 tonne payload is under development, with a first test launch planned for 2021. There are plans to use it to launch a lunar orbiter in 2023, and a lunar lander in 2025. South Korea is also a world leader in many of the other civilian technologies that would be useful for a nuclear-weapons programme, including semiconductors, precision machine tools and high-energy conventional explosives.

However, South Korea does not possess either of the sensitive technologies necessary for fissile-material production. This is not for lack of trying. As well as conducting weapons programmes in the 1970s, South Korea has intermittently sought reprocessing technologies for nearly 50 years, for reasons of both energy security and national pride. South Korea's original purpose for reprocessing, as reflected in a 1968 long-term energy plan, was to fuel fast-breeder reactors. In the late 1980s, recycling plutonium was seen as a way to reduce dependence on imported uranium. In the 1990s, the rationale shifted to addressing problems with disposing of spent fuel.[39] Like other countries, South Korea has no central repository; by law, spent fuel must be stored on the site at which it was irradiated, and some sites in the country will reportedly run out of storage capacity by 2016.[40] Energy independence also remains an important motivation. The ROK has identified nuclear energy as a major profitable export sector, and sees the area as reliant on technological independence.[41] South Koreans also assert that if they do not recycle plutonium, they lose the economic potential of spent fuel (even though no country has yet been able to harness that economic potential).

A less focused desire for enrichment became evident in the 1990s. Enrichment technology did not feature in the 1970s weapons programmes, nor in civilian research programmes until the AVLIS experiments conducted by KAERI from 1993–2000. It came as a surprise when, in negotiations that began in 2010 over renewing the US–ROK bilateral nuclear-cooperation agreement, South Korean officials said that, in addition to the right to recycle US-supplied fuel using a technology called pyroprocessing (see below), they also wanted US consent for enrichment.[42] South Korea's nuclear complex is large enough to make indigenous enrichment economical, in theory. The ability to provide enriched fuel, some claim, would also make exporting South Korean nuclear power plants more competitive. Unspoken in most public discourse is the weapons-hedging option that enrichment would provide.

When South Koreans speak of the need for nuclear independence, they often present enrichment and reprocessing as necessary to this goal. The desire is encapsulated in the slogan 'peaceful nuclear sovereignty'. But the origin of the phrase gives it problematic connotations. In the 1970s, the term 'nuclear sovereignty' was a euphemism for developing nuclear weapons. As American nuclear experts Toby Dalton and Alexandra Francis explain, adding 'peaceful' to the term does not change the original idea: a 'desire to exercise more control over the scope of its nuclear energy activities and shed what is seen as an unwelcome level of US control'.[43]

The quest for nuclear independence is fuelled by emotive nationalism and resentment over discrimination. South Koreans are galled that Japan is allowed to reprocess plutonium and enrich uranium, while the ROK is not. For example, many South Koreans saw as unfair the criticism levelled at the ROK in 2004 for small-scale enrichment and reprocessing experiments, in light of global acquiescence to Japan's possession of a huge plutonium stockpile.[44] South Korea's sense of unfairness was exacerbated by the change to US law that permitted nuclear commerce with India – which is not party to the NPT – and the latter's use of US uranium in sensitive technologies. Most recently, South Koreans have commented that even Iran is allowed uranium enrichment (albeit not for US-obligated nuclear material). The fact that Switzerland can send spent fuel to France for reprocessing and receive the resulting plutonium has also been cited as an example of unequal treatment. South Koreans plaintively insist that they have advanced technologically and politically to the point at which they are owed the same rights. Unlike India, Iran and Switzerland, the ROK is a first-tier US ally and thus should be treated as an equal of Japan, goes the argument. 'Why don't you trust us?' is an oft-heard refrain.

South Koreans are generally unconvinced by the reasons given for the differences. Japan got its foot in the door by investing in reprocessing and enrichment before the US changed its policy to oppose the spread of these technologies (see Chapter Two). Moreover, unlike South Korea, Japan did not seek to use these technologies for weapons purposes after the Second World War, and has a spotless record in honouring its IAEA-safeguards obligations.

Given South Korea's history of weapons development and the support for nuclear armament among a sizable portion of the population, the state's desire for sensitive nuclear technologies is suspected of being a nuclear-hedging strategy. Some South Koreans undermine their case for plutonium recycling when they argue that having a reprocessing capability would enhance the nation's nuclear diplomacy. After insisting that the ROK would only use the technology for civilian purposes, two separate South Korean national-security experts have said privately that China, fearing South Korea could use the technology for nuclear weapons, would have greater reason to pressure North Korea to denuclearise.[45] At a seminar held in Washington DC in October 2014, commentator Moon Chang-keuk, who earlier in the year emerged as a prime-ministerial candidate, said South Korea needs to be a 'nuclear technology' state. Living next to nuclear-armed China and North Korea, South Korea should also have the capability, although without acquiring a nuclear weapon for now, he said. According to a former senior US diplomat, 'when they talk about pyropro-cessing, a lot of South Korean security thinkers have weapons in mind.'[46] One former ROK cabinet minister said that govern-ment interest in enrichment and reprocessing was sparked by the first signs, in 1989, of North Korea's nuclear-related explosives tests.[47] This is not to deny the power of economic motivations, which are probably dominant, but the hedging strategy is also a significant factor.

Negotiations over the renewal of the 1974 US–ROK nuclear-cooperation agreement (often called a '123 Agreement', after Section 123 of the US Atomic Energy Act, which establishes conditions for nuclear cooperation) lasted five years before being concluded in April 2015. The new 20-year agreement did not provide Washington's consent in advance for the enrich-ment or recycling of US-supplied fuel, but also did not rule out these technologies, allowing the ROK government to save face.

The most contentious issue was South Korea's desire for plutonium recycling through pyroprocessing. Unlike the more common PUREX reprocessing method, which uses liquid solvents to separate pure plutonium from spent fuel, pyro-processing results in plutonium that is still mixed with other transuranic elements, including americium and neptunium, and thus not immediately usable for weapons. ROK officials contend that this makes pyroprocessing more proliferation-resistant, but US government experts do not see a substantial difference, on grounds that pyroprocessing could be used to create weapons-grade plutonium if the process were taken a step further.

The US worries that possessing this technology and gaining experience in working with metal fuel would considerably shorten the time it would take South Korea to build a nuclear weapon. The concern is not specific to South Korea. With limited exceptions, all of Washington's 123 agreements restrict the enrichment and reprocessing of US-origin nuclear material. The US is keen to avoid making exceptions that would set precedents for other states. In the case of South Korea, there is also a concern that allowing either enrichment or a form of reprocessing, in contravention of the 1992 North–South denuclearisation agreement, would make it even more difficult to persuade North Korea to return to the conditions of that accord.[48]

Although ROK President Park Geun-hye raised the issue with US President Barack Obama in April 2014, he held to non-proliferation principles, in contrast to the earlier decision to allow an extension of the range of ROK missiles. The US and South Korea will continue to review pyroprocessing as part of a ten-year fuel-cycle study that began in 2011. Scientists from the two nations are jointly investigating the technical feasibility of pyroprocessing, its prospects for industrial-scale deployment and its proliferation implications.[49] In effect, the issue has been put off until 2021. Meanwhile, South Korea is allowed to send its spent fuel to France for reprocessing, although the return of this material in the form of mixed-oxide fuel will still be subject to US consent. As for uranium enrichment, the US will facilitate South Korean investment in a multilateral enrichment consortium in Europe or North America.

Unlike earlier such deals with the UAE and Taiwan, the 123 agreement with South Korea did not require the country to adopt the so-called gold standard: renouncing enrichment and reprocessing. And, as with the US–Vietnam 123 agreement, the ROK was not asked to make a political statement implicitly renouncing these technologies. Former State Department senior official Robert Einhorn, who at one stage led the talks with South Korea, explained that the US position on pyroprocessing was not 'no, never', but 'no, not now'. He added that the agreement contains 'unique elements that the US has not been prepared to accept with any other nuclear partners [sic]'.[50]

Postponing the pyroprocessing issue gives the ROK more time also to address the technological challenges associated with its strategy for managing spent fuel. Pyroprocessing was only to be the first step in the recycling plan. The next stage would be to irradiate the transuranic elements in fast reactors, which are still under development. Pyroprocessing might someday be an answer to South Korea's problems in spent-fuel management, but not for several decades. In the meantime, regulations will have to be changed to allow interim dry-cask storage, inter-site transhipment and, ideally, direct disposal in deep repositories.

What if?

Today, South Korea shows no sign of revisiting its past nuclear-weapons pursuit, and the preponderance of reasons for holding to this path is likely to keep the government true to its non-proliferation commitments. If the relevant constraints were to change, however, it is worth asking how long it would take South Korea to build a bomb.

Given its industrial might, large pool of nuclear engineers and scientists, and the speed with which it has mastered other nuclear technologies, the ROK would face few technical barriers to producing a bomb. Its past weaponisation work, and perhaps also its small-scale experiments in enrichment and reprocessing, would give the country a head start. Yet it lacks dedicated facilities for either enrichment or reprocessing. The latter provides the quicker route, and could enable the production of a bomb in two years or less.

In theory, a small reprocessing plant could be built quickly. In 1977 the US Oak Ridge National Laboratory concluded that, under certain conditions, a simple reprocessing plant could be built in as little as four to six months, and that the first 10kg of plutonium could be recovered about a week after the facility began operations. This estimate did not take into account steps such as plant design, the recruitment and training of staff, or the need for post-construction testing, which together would increase the estimated time it would take to begin operations to 19–24 months or longer.[51] The estimate of four to six months may also have been based on the presumption that engineers would first be able to surreptitiously extract low burn-up fuel from South Korea's heavy-water reactors.[52] Taking a more cautious approach, one Korean scholar estimated in 1978 that it would take South Korea four to six years to build a bomb, taking into account not only fissile-material production but also the effort to design and fashion a weapon, as well as related activity.[53] US strategic-weapons expert James Clay Moltz concluded in 2006 that it would take South Korea at least a year to separate enough plutonium for a weapon.[54]

In the normal run of things, Moltz is probably correct. In dire circumstances, however, South Korea could also use low burn-up spent fuel already on hand. Without the need to build a dedicated reprocessing facility, small amounts of plutonium could be separated at the nine hot cells at KAERI's Irradiated Material Examination Facility near Daejeon. This facility is not designed to separate plutonium, but it could be adapted to do so. With this concern in mind, the US insisted that the ROK limit the size of the KAERI hot cells.[55]

It must be emphasised that none of these steps to producing fissile material for a weapon could be taken without the awareness of the IAEA. A weapons path would only be taken if Seoul had no concern for secrecy, NPT commitments or alliance obligations, as discussed below.

Non-proliferation policy and contrary public opinion

Seemingly determined to burnish its non-proliferation credentials after the 2004 revelations, South Korea has in the past decade taken prominent roles in several international efforts. In 2007, for example, Seoul joined the Global Initiative to Combat Nuclear Terrorism, and in 2011 hosted the organisation's plenary meeting. In 2009 Seoul became an active participant in the US-led Proliferation Security Initiative, and the next year joined the organisation's Operational Experts Group, the policymaking body for the initiative.[56] In 2012 president Lee Myung-bak hosted the second Nuclear Security Summit. The ROK had become a member of the Nuclear Suppliers Group (NSG) and the Zangger Committee in 1995, and had signed the Convention on Physical Protection of Nuclear Material in 1982. In 2016–17, South Korea will chair the NSG for a second time.

South Korea also cooperates closely with the US on nonproliferation issues at several levels. US–Korea bilateral consultations on disarmament and non-proliferation have taken place annually since 2013. In January 2015, the two countries quietly began director-level talks on counter-proliferation. In support of US-led sanctions against Iran, the ROK steadily reduced its oil purchases from the country between 2012 and 2014.

Although Seoul's policies in support of non-proliferation remain strong, popular attitudes are surprisingly contrary. Over the past two decades, most opinion polls have found that a clear majority of South Koreans back indigenous nuclear-weapons development. Widely publicised polls conducted in 2012 and 2013 by the Asan Institute for Policy Studies found that two-thirds of the population supported nuclearisation.[57] Although some critics discount these polls because the founder of the Asan Institute, Chung Mong-joon, is South Korea's most vocal advocate of nuclear weapons, they are consistent with research by other organisations. According to a poll conducted by Realmeter and tv-N in March 2011, for example, 72.5% of the public supported South Korean nuclearisation.[58] Two polls carried out in 2013 found that there was 64% and 62% support.[59]

These studies are also in line with previous surveys, albeit with some fluctuation in the numbers. A poll taken in September 2005 by *Joongang Ilbo* and the East Asia Institute found 66.5% of South Koreans believed that the ROK should possess nuclear weapons, although one year earlier another poll registered 51% support.[60] In polls taken in 1996 and 1999 by the RAND Center for Asia-Pacific Policy and *Joongang Ilbo*, 91% and 82% respectively agreed that, if North Korea had nuclear weapons, South Korea should acquire them too. Even higher numbers of people – 92.5% in 1996 and 87% in 1999 – said South Korea should acquire nuclear weapons if Japan acquired them.[61] While it appears that support for nuclearisation is lower today than it was in the 1990s, it is noteworthy that such support has been over 50% in every poll. The surveys demonstrate the consistent weakness of the non-proliferation norm in South Korea.

As a less provocative and more easily reversible alternative to indigenous nuclearisation, some South Koreans contend that the same purpose of responding to North Korea could be served through the reintroduction of US nuclear weapons, which were withdrawn in 1991. In a 2012 essay, political scientist Cheon Seong-whun argued that redeploying a modest number of US tactical nuclear weapons 'would provide a trump card that would enable a breakthrough in the North Korean nuclear problem'.[62] Others have contended that the physical presence of US weapons would make nuclear deterrence more credible, and allow the US to strike North Korean targets more quickly.[63] The same public-opinion polls that register strong support for domestic nuclear weapons find nearly the same level of support for the return of US weapons.[64] Some members of the US Congress have expressed support for reconsidering the removal of US nuclear forces from South Korea, but neither the Obama administration nor the Pentagon have expressed any interest in revisiting the matter.[65]

ROK government officials downplay the significance of pro-nuclear poll results on grounds that support for nuclear weapons is as shallow as it is wide, representing little more than a nationalistic impulse to counter North Korea. In autumn 2014, the Ministry of Foreign Affairs commissioned a poll that asked respondents if they would support nuclearisation knowing that the consequences would involve economic sanctions and international disapprobation. Under these circumstances, support fell below 50%. The poll results convinced ministry officials of the need for more non-proliferation education in South Korea.[66]

There are strong advocates for nuclearisation, including Kim Dae-joong and other columnists at the conservative *Chosun Ilbo* newspaper. Such calls pay no heed to the nation's obligations under the NPT. This is a new phenomenon; pro-nuclearisation views were not heard from establishment figures a decade ago, before North Korea's first nuclear test.[67] Today's calls for nuclear weapons are an expression of frustration that nothing else has worked to restrain Pyongyang. It would be wrong, however, to infer from this that there is a fervent pro-nuclear campaign under way. A 2013 study by the Washington-based Carnegie Endowment for International Peace concluded: 'public opinion seems to reflect a general sense of insecurity among South Koreans more than a real desire that their government build nuclear weapons.'[68] Those who understand the implications, costs and downsides of an indigenous nuclear-weapons programme are far less supportive.[69]

Proliferation drivers

North Korea's nuclear tests and robust missile programme underscore its repeated threats to turn Seoul into a 'sea of fire'.[70] Although the ROK government is reluctant to conclude that DPRK nuclear warheads can be mounted on the missiles, it seems highly probable that they can be, given that North Korea has been working on weaponisation for nearly 30 years. Nuclear weapons have been enshrined in the North Korean constitution and, insist DPRK officials, will never be traded away.[71] Some South Koreans are concerned that the US is willing to acquiesce to the DPRK's nuclear-armed status, and to instead focus on containment, preventing North Korea from exporting its nuclear-weapons technology. South Korea, on the other hand, cannot ignore the nuclear nightmare Pyongyang evokes.[72]

North Korea possesses about 1,000 *Scud* and *Nodong* ballistic missiles capable of reaching anywhere in South Korea. It also has about 100 mobile launchers for these missiles,[73] and has carried out multiple test launches. Judging by the operations of its reactors and its reprocessing activities, North Korea has plutonium sufficient for as many as ten nuclear weapons. After a hiatus between 2007 and 2014, plutonium production resumed. In 2013 one of the country's uranium-enrichment facilities doubled its floor space, potentially allowing it to add to this stockpile. Joel Wit and other US experts believe that, by 2020, North Korea could have 20–100 nuclear weapons.[74] Some Chinese experts believe that North Korea already has 20 warheads, and could build 20 more by 2016.[75] These assessments create the perception of a security gap; thus, South Korea needs nuclear weapons to restore the balance of power, runs the popular argument. And numbers matter. Missile-defence systems might be effective against a small number of incoming missiles. Pre-emptive strikes might also be able to knock out a small number of nuclear-armed missiles. The ROK plans to make use of both approaches, using conventional missiles as part of a 'kill chain' system. Against a large number of missiles, however, such defences are less viable.

After North Korea's second nuclear test, in May 2009, some members of parliament, generally those from the ruling Grand National Party (now named the Saenuri Party), began to call for the government to consider acquiring indigenous nuclear weapons as a deterrent against the North Korean nuclear threat. Saenuri parliamentary leaders repeated the call after North Korea's fourth nuclear test on 6 January 2015. Nonetheless, the overall South Korean response to the North's nuclear tests has been muted and sober. North Korea's nuclear tests did not prompt any major changes in government policy, apart from an increase in sanctions against the North, nor an inflamed rhetorical response.

Nuclearisation advocates argue that, in addition to restoring deterrence, balancing the North's nuclear arsenal would also improve Seoul's bargaining power. As Chung put it, 'the threat of a nuclear counterforce may be the only way to change the North's perception of the South.'[76] He and other advocates also contend that an ROK nuclear-weapons programme would create leverage vis-à-vis China, giving Beijing a reason to put pressure on Pyongyang to negotiate denuclearisation. As explained by one of his associates: 'the suggestion to develop South Korea's own nuclear weapons was a negotiation ploy. The purpose is not for the ROK to have nuclear weapons. Chung wants others – China and the US – to pay attention and do something about [North Korea's] nuclear programme.'[77]

The fault in this approach is that China seems unwilling under any circumstances to exert pressure that could cause cracks in the North Korean regime. Even in unofficial discussions, Chinese participants decline to discuss potential cooperation to manage the consequences of a North Korean collapse, lest it become a self-fulfilling prophecy and create trouble on China's border.

Some South Korean nuclear advocates argue that visibly heading down the nuclear-weapons path would also put pressure on Washington and Moscow to put more effort into persuading North Korea to retreat.[78] Such an approach, known in political science as an 'instrumentalist' use of the nuclear option, was probably taken by Park Chung-hee in his resumed pursuit of nuclear weapons in the late 1970s.[79] A similar intention could be inferred from President Park Geun-hye's comment in an 18 May 2014 interview with the *Wall Street Journal* that a fourth North Korean nuclear test could spark a 'nuclear domino effect' in Northeast Asia.[80] She also reportedly made a comment along these lines during a telephone call with Chinese President Xi Jinping the previous month.[81] Although directed foremost at Beijing, her reference to a nuclear arms race was also a strategic reminder to Washington.

If North Korea's nuclear programme expands dramatically, in line with Wit's worst-case scenario, the possibility of it provoking a South Korean nuclear push cannot be discounted. South Korea has faced a North Korean military threat for so many years that the population has generally come to accept it as normal. Seoul, in particular, is within range of hundreds of North Korea's long-range artillery pieces. Yet public threat perceptions could change if the nuclear overhang becomes demonstrably worse – both quantitatively, in terms of arsenal size, and qualitatively, if the North successfully tests new kinds of nuclear weapons and missile re-entry vehicles.

Credibility of US extended deterrence

The nuclear imbalance between North and South Korea is not relevant unless one doubts the credibility of US extended deterrence. Most South Koreans have faith in the alliance. Polling by the Asan Institute in March 2014 showed support for the alliance at 93%, nearly an all-time high.[82] The anti-American angst that used to be so common in leftist circles has largely faded. A group of US experts on Asia who visited South Korea in autumn 2014, for example, heard consistent praise for the state of relations. According to their trip report: 'cooperation at all levels of the relationship is strong, channels of communication are numerous and active, and there is a shared view among US and ROK alliance managers that the relationship has never been better.'[83] Attitudes have undergone a significant change since as recently as a decade ago, when foreign-policy scholars Jonathan Pollack and Mitchell Reiss assessed that the alliance was 'experiencing severe strain'.[84]

The presence of US Forces Korea, the size of which has remained at about 28,500 personnel since 2006, is a visible manifestation of the American commitment. Compared to the 1970s, there now is far less concern about the possibility of US troops withdrawing. Still, Koreans have deeper anxieties about US abandonment than, for example, the Japanese.[85] The concern is: 'will the US be ready to sacrifice Los Angeles to save Seoul?', as one South Korean scholar put it.[86] This is the Korean equivalent of the decoupling question Charles de Gaulle raised in the late 1950s about US willingness to trade New York for Paris. North Korea today may not be able to hit US cities with nuclear-armed missiles, but it is working hard to establish this capability by developing road-mobile KN-08 ICBMs and submarine-launched ballistic missiles. In April 2015, the head of the North American Aerospace Defense Command said US intelligence believed that North Korea was capable of mounting a miniaturised nuclear weapon on the KN-08 and firing it at the US.[87] This assessment was based on prudence in planning for the worst. Because the KN-08 has never been flight tested, its capabilities are unknown. North Korea is also developing road-mobile *Musudan* missiles that have a potential range of 4,000km, which would put Guam in reach, although that system has not been flight tested either.

If North Korea does prove that it has a working ICBM, the 'de Gaulle question' will become newly prominent. The decoupling concern will be ameliorated, however, if the US has effective missile defences against a potential North Korean ICBM. This factor is cited among the arguments for basing a Terminal High Altitude Area Defense (THAAD) system in South Korea, although South Korea has been cautious about THAAD because of China's strong objections to the move. In the meantime, North Korea's capabilities should not be exaggerated, especially in the absence of systems that have been successfully tested, including re-entry vehicles.

Some South Koreans see signs that the US is ready to acquiesce to North Korea's nuclear-armed status, as long as Pyongyang keeps the weapons on the peninsula and does not help any outside player, such as Iran or terrorist groups, with technology or material related to such arms. The US government maintains that, like the ROK, it will not accept North Korea as a nuclear-armed state and will always insist on denuclearisation. Any change to this policy would exacerbate fears of abandonment.

They are not the only factors, but the health and credibility of the US–ROK alliance is related to South Koreans' inclination to go nuclear.[88] Pointing to the high support for indigenous nuclear weapons among South Koreans in polls, nuclear-policy analyst John Park suggests that public opinion must reflect questions about the credibility of US extended-deterrence guarantees.[89] Some South Koreans doubt whether Washington would use nuclear weapons if their security were imperilled. Some invoke the image of a torn nuclear umbrella. But few would want nuclear war on the peninsula, and South Koreans realise that US extended deterrence includes powerful conventional forces.

A stronger argument is that extended deterrence has not proven useful in stopping North Korea's nuclear programme or rhetorical threats. Conservative scholar Kim Taewoo argues that 'extended deterrence deters nuclear weapons, not nuclear blackmail'.[90] Nor has US deterrence prevented North Korean small-scale conventional provocations, which was never its purpose. A sense that the US has been ineffective is behind the desire to take matters into one's own hands with a nuclear-weapons programme.

Several US moves in the diplomatic, defence and economic realms have helped to reassure South Koreans, who welcomed Obama's policy of 'rebalancing' to Asia as evidence of sustained commitment to the alliance.[91] The security dialogue has been strengthened at several levels. At a 2009 summit, the Joint Vision of the Alliance statement signed by presidents Obama and Lee referred to 'the continuing commitment of extended deterrence, including the US nuclear umbrella', words that were included as a means of reassurance at the ROK's request. US–ROK Security Consultative Meetings also regularly include references to the nuclear umbrella. Since 2010, the US and ROK foreign and defence ministers and secretaries have jointly held three '2+2' ministerial meetings. At the working level, a biannual Korea–US Integrated Defense Dialogue was established in 2011 to coordinate defence strategy, and an inter-agency Extended Deterrence Policy Committee was initiated in 2010 for consultations on US–ROK responses to North Korean threats. In addition to policy discussions, the dialogue includes table-top exercises involving simulations of North Korean use of nuclear weapons and visits to bases hosting nuclear forces.[92] In 2015 it was renamed the 'Deterrence Strategy Committee' in order to convey the idea that deterrence is undertaken by both allies as a mutual endeavour.

The entry into force of the US–Korea free-trade agreement in March 2012 strengthened the economic component of the relationship. Military ties have also been visibly enhanced. In March 2013, after North Korea bombastically threatened to carry out a nuclear attack on American cities, the Pentagon made a point of publicising training missions in South Korean airspace by B-52 bombers and B-2 fighter-bombers, both of which are nuclear-capable. Their purpose was as much to reassure South Korea of American resolve as to warn and deter the North. The US decision in 2012 to accept Seoul's plans to extend the range of its missiles to 800km was also made as a means of reassurance that Washington understands South Korean security concerns.

There should be no doubt about American capacity to help defend South Korea. In addition to the B-52 and B-2 bombers, US submarine-launched and land-based missiles could obliterate any North Korean target within minutes. Conventional precision-strike weapons and bunker busters could also be used to accomplish most military operations against the North. Conventional weapons are also a more credible deterrent, given the 'proportionality' norm of just war and the long-standing taboo against nuclear-weapon use.

Other potential proliferation triggers

Most South Koreans believe that, if Japan was to acquire nuclear weapons, they would need to do the same.[93] Due to historical animosities, Koreans (and Chinese) are intensely suspicious of Japan, and are certain that Prime Minister Shinzo

Abe is leading his nation down the path to remilitarisation. They are convinced that Japan, with its enrichment and reprocessing capabilities and advanced aerospace technology, could go nuclear at a moment's notice, and that it is simply a matter of time before the country takes this path.[94] As previously mentioned, in South Korea, resentment runs deep over the perceived unfairness that the US has allowed Japan, but not the ROK, to possess sensitive nuclear technology. According to one former ROK cabinet minister, when South Koreans say they need nuclear weapons, it is Japan as much as North Korea that they have in mind as a threat.[95] This view is partly based on relative economic strength. Judging itself to be far superior to the North in every category save strategic weapons, South Korea sees Japan as its primary peer competitor.[96]

Emotional nationalism also comes into play. Speaking with irony, former national security advisor Chun Yungwoo responded to A-bomb advocates: 'if Japan went nuclear, so would we; if Japan takes poison, we would take poison, too.'[97] Even South Korean officials make little effort to hide their distrust. One senior ROK official was quoted in 2014 as saying, 'South Korea wouldn't care how many nuclear weapons China acquires, or even if the North Koreans develop several more (nukes) … as long as Japan does not become nuclear!'[98]

Negative attitudes are hardening. In recent polls, 70% of South Koreans express an unfavourable view of Japan. Beyond dislike, they are becoming more apt to feel threatened. A 2014 survey found that 46% of South Koreans view Japan as a military threat and 41% believe that their country will be involved in a military conflict with Japan in the future.[99] A perceived need to prepare for that eventuality underpins pro-nuclear attitudes in South Korea. If Japan were to acquire nuclear weapons, it would be to target nuclear-armed adversaries, not the ROK. Yet South Koreans would see such weapons as a threat. This is not entirely irrational: while intentions may change, geography does not. If Japan were to go nuclear and American forces were to withdraw from the region, South Korea would not want to be left as the only non-nuclear state in the region.

As US expert on East Asia Scott Snyder comments, as long as ROK–Japan relations remain cordial and Japan does not abandon its non-nuclear policy, background resentment and animosities will not trigger a South Korean push for nuclearisation.[100] Moreover, anti-Japanese views are not immutable. Half of respondents to a 2014 Asan Institute poll were supportive of an ROK–Japan summit and of signing a low-level agreement with Japan to share intelligence about North Korea, which had been delayed due to political opposition. A clear majority – 64% – said that security cooperation with Japan would be a necessity if China continued to rise.[101] In December 2014, the ROK, Japan and the US signed a three-way agreement to share intelligence on the DPRK, with the US acting as a conduit between Japan and the ROK.

Today, South Koreans do not fear China per se. On the contrary, over the past two decades ROK–China relations have become remarkably amicable. A far cry from its days as a Korean War foe, China is now South Korea's top trading partner and source of tourists. Under Park Geun-hye, the rapprochement has deepened. Asan Institute polls taken in 2014 found popular support for China among South Koreans to be at its highest level ever. The polls also found, however, that 'wariness of China lingers just below the surface'. Koreans view the increase in China's hard power as an indirect threat because it makes the region more dangerous. An ROK–China territorial dispute over the submerged Socotra Rock (Ieodo/ Suyanjiao), south of Jeju Island, flared up in 2006 and remains unresolved. South Koreans also are dissatisfied with China's posture on North Korea. They want Beijing to do more to stop

Pyongyang's provocations, and believe that China does not support Korean unification.[102] Beijing's 'coddling' of North Korea over the deadly provocations in 2010 was seen as empowering Pyongyang's bad behaviour. Frustration with China contributes to the popular belief that Seoul should threaten to go nuclear in order to send a message to Beijing.

Nationalism was a secondary but significant factor in Park Chung-hee's pursuit of nuclear weapons. For him, A-bombs were a symbol of autonomy and self-reliance.[103] This sentiment remains a motivation today. As the head of a South Korean think tank explained, 'the context of the popular desire for nuclear weapons is that we have to stand on our own feet and escape being a shrimp among whales.'[104]

In comparison to other states that might be considered potential nuclear dominoes, South Korea is in the unique position of possibly inheriting nuclear weapons, in the event of unification with the North. ROK leaders have emphasised that a unified Korea will be nuclear-weapons free.[105] The North's weapons would be dismantled and the unified nation would retain South Korea's status as a non-nuclear-weapons state party to the NPT. If this were not the clear policy, Korea's neighbours and Western partners would surely oppose unification. Yet the circumstances of unification are unpredictable. While an orderly process would allow for the careful dismantlement of the weapons and international verification, an abrupt collapse of the DPRK government and the need for prompt action to secure nuclear assets before they found their way onto the black market or into the hands of warlords could leave doubts about whether they had all been destroyed. There might be a powerful temptation to keep some nuclear arms. As Pollack and Reiss put it, 'the impulse to seek or continue national advantage through independent strategic capacities could prove irresistible to a unified Korea.'[106]

Even if all weapons, fissile materials and production facilities were dismantled under the watch of international monitors, presumably a unified Korea would retain the weapons-related expertise of the scientists and engineers who were involved in the programme. There would be a need for an effort to redirect these experts into suitable civilian occupations, akin to that which established the International Science and Technology Center after the fall of the Soviet Union.

It is possible that reunification could end the US–ROK alliance, for two reasons: China would be unlikely to accept the presence of a US ally on its eastern land border; and US Forces Korea would have lost its primary mission, providing a defence against the DPRK. Lacking an alliance with Washington, future Korean leaders might look to nuclear weapons as an alternative insurance policy. On the other hand, they might realise that retaining nuclear-weapons capabilities could spur an arms race with Japan at the same time as it imperilled relations with both China and the US.

Nationalism may be the determining factor. Nationalistic pride in nuclear achievements is felt on both sides of the 38th parallel. *Mugunwha Gatchi Piyosumnida* (*Rose of Sharon Blooms Again*), a popular ultranationalist novel published in 1991, tells the story of a fictional South Korean scientist in the Park era who secretly helps North Korea develop nuclear weapons, which the two Koreas then deploy to ward off Japanese aggression.[107] Such fantasies are not limited to popular culture. Leftist South Korean intellectuals are known to have discussed reunification in neo-nationalist terms, depicting a unified peninsula that is both independent of American protection and nuclear-armed.[108]

Nonetheless, in the South Korean security community, there is a widespread belief that the US alliance will continue after unification. Given their historical experience of being surrounded by larger powers, most Koreans know they will still need a strong extra-regional ally and that the alliance would not be easily compatible with indigenous nuclear weapons.

Constraints

The high level of popular support for nuclear-weapons development reflected in opinion polls does not mean that South Korea as a state has ambitions to go down this path again. The government's non-proliferation policy is firm. Officials know that departing from it would have marginal benefits and huge economic and security costs. As a move intended to enhance South Korean security, it would be highly counterproductive. Although some scenarios for going nuclear are plausible, most are not, especially in light of South Korea's democratic system and free press. In the foreseeable future, South Korea's pursuit of nuclear weapons is thus highly unlikely.

Pursuing nuclear weapons would be disastrous for South Korea's nuclear-energy programme, which provides 29% of the nation's power. The supply of uranium fuel to the nation's reactors would be cut off under the terms of bilateral nuclear-cooperation agreements with the US, France and other states. Facilities for fuel fabrication, nuclear research, medical-isotope production and other nuclear-science purposes would all be affected, putting at risk assets worth several hundred billion dollars.[109] South Korea's US$40bn contract to construct and manage four US-designed nuclear power plants in the UAE would also be threatened, and the nation's high hopes for becoming a leading nuclear-technology exporter would wither.

Apart from the civilian nuclear-energy industry, the impact on trade is hard to quantify. If South Korea sought nuclear arms after first exercising its Article X right to withdraw from the NPT because 'extraordinary events have jeopardized [its] supreme interests', then it would not be violating any international treaty that would automatically trigger wide-spread penalties. Its trading partners still might apply various economic sanctions, perhaps in the order of those levelled against India and Pakistan after their 1998 nuclear tests. In that case, US law required the termination of non-humanitarian assistance, defence sales and credit guarantees, as well as opposition to lending by international financial institutions. Japan froze new loans and grants to the countries, and a few other nations suspended aid and credit lines. Most of the US sanctions were lifted within a few months, and they were almost entirely removed in three years.[110] It should be noted, however, that South Korea's economy is more dependent on foreign trade than was India's, and is thus more vulnerable to sanctions. From 2011 to 2013, for example, South Korea's ratio of exports and imports to gross national income exceeded 100%, the highest among the G20 nations. The economic impact of even partial sanctions that reduced access to trade, finance and investment markets would be substantial. Even in the 1970s, consideration of the damage to the South Korean economy was a major reason president Park Chung-hee stopped his pursuit of nuclear weapons after it had been exposed.[111]

Even more damaging than the economic fallout would be the negative implications for national security. As with Park's nuclear-weapons programme, a decision to go nuclear today would threaten an alliance that has been fundamental to South Korea's security. Revocation of the US deterrence commitment would be by no means inevitable,[112] but prudent ROK security planners would have to assume the worst: a future US administration would respond the same way that Kissinger did in the 1970s. The claim by some South Korean nuclear advocates that the US is only opposed to its 'enemies' having nuclear weapons is wrong.[113] Washington would have a strong reason to once again oppose the development of an independent nuclear force that would upend the global non-proliferation regime, and that could entangle America in a nuclear conflict. ROK political scientist Moon Chung-in argues that 'no US Commander-in-Chief is going to put American forces in harm's way in a Korean conflict, if South Korea wields nuclear weapons outside of US political and military command-and-control.'[114] Even if it was not broken, the alliance would come under severe strain.

Resumed pursuit of nuclear weapons would make South Korea intensely vulnerable in the period before it produced and fielded deliverable nuclear weapons. Given the nation's open political system, rambunctious press and undisciplined legislature, it would be nearly impossible to hide a nuclear-weapons programme. Even Park Chung-hee's authoritarian government, which ruled with little transparency, was unable to keep his programme secret from prying American eyes. In today's vibrant and adversarial democracy, the parliamentary oversight and funding authorisation required for such a programme would be liable to expose it to a legislative body notorious for disclosing secrets. Nuclear activity would also be hard to keep from the IAEA, with its well-practised access rights under the Additional Protocol.[115] In fact, most South Koreans who advocate an indigenous nuclear programme expressly want any such effort to be public knowledge, in order to put diplomatic pressure on China and other external actors.

If South Korea persisted with such a programme after its discovery, North Korea would see this as a hostile move, and perhaps be tempted to launch a pre-emptive attack at a time when the US defence commitment might no longer apply. Short of this worst-case scenario, North Korea would claim the South's actions as a justification for stepping up its own weapons programme, which was accelerated in response to Park's 1970s pursuit of nuclear arms.[116] The idea that Seoul's acquisition of nuclear weapons would pressure Pyongyang to negotiate an end to its own nuclear programme involves a desperate gamble. It is more likely that denuclearising North Korea would become even more difficult than it is today. And, if South Korea were to acquire nuclear weapons or resume hosting US tactical nuclear weapons for negotiations that did not succeed, under what conditions could they be given up without signalling defeat? The peninsula would be left with an enduring nuclear stand-off.

In addition to North Korea, other neighbouring nations would have ample reasons for viewing South Korean nucle-arisation with anxiety. Russia and China could be expected, as a matter of course, to target the weapons facilities.[117] Japan, as the only non-nuclear state in the region, could be prompted to reconsider its own weapons option, and in doing so Tokyo would have a large head start over Seoul. As foreign-policy scholars Choi Kang and Park Joon-sung have noted, 'the nuclear domino game is not a "winnable" one from a South Korean viewpoint.'[118] In short, if South Korea went nuclear, the Korean Peninsula and its environs would become much more tense and dangerous. The ensuing economic impact from capital flight, postponed investment and stock-market depression could be even more adverse than the direct impact of sanctions. It is hard to envisage circumstances in which US tactical nuclear weapons could be returned to South Korea. American officials, both civilian and military, are thoroughly opposed to the idea for very good reasons. The operational requirements of housing the weapons, which would include hardened bunkers and special security units, would impose new burdens on overstretched military budgets. The bases containing the systems would be targets for a potential North Korean pre-emptive attack, possibly one involving commando forces. Seizure by terrorists would be another concern. The weapons themselves are unnecessary; they have no military use that could not be served by either conventional weapons or US strategic nuclear weapons launched from submarines, missiles or long-range bombers. As is the case with US tactical nuclear weapons stationed in Europe, their purpose would be solely symbolic. But the symbolism would be double-edged. China and Russia would see it as a provocation, and North Korea might find greater sympathy abroad. At home, the weapons would reignite anti-American protests, reopening domestic divisions that would undermine bilateral relations. Before the US weapons were withdrawn in 1991, their removal was a key rallying point for South Korea's pro-democracy movement. Recalling this experience, South Korean officials have not asked for the weapons to return.

The other costs of going nuclear include damage to the ROK's international image, and its standing as a leading global citizen. As was arguably the case with India, prestige can be a motivation for acquiring nuclear weapons. For South Korea, prestige considerations play to the desire to possess the same sensitive nuclear technologies employed by Japan. The ROK already enjoys a high level of respect internationally, however. The country now has the world's 13th-largest economy, a powerful advanced-technology sector and a popular culture of global renown. Its citizens lead the United Nations and the World Bank, and it has hosted key events, such as the 2012 Nuclear Security Summit. Establishing a nuclear-weapons programme, in contravention of its commitment to the NPT and against the strong expectations of its main ally and other global partners, would undermine South Korea's status as a leading 'middle power'. A nuclear South Korea might not be regarded as a 'rogue state', but its movement in that direction would be precipitous. The country would lose the moral high ground vis-à-vis North Korea, and would find it harder to sustain international sanctions against Pyongyang.[119] The cause of unification would be seriously undermined, with the stand-off on the peninsula sharply escalating.

Assessment

For South Korea, going nuclear would be foolhardy for both economic and security reasons, in equal measures counterproductive and unnecessary. Reintroducing US nuclear weapons would also be unwise. No purpose could be served by positioning nuclear weapons (indigenous or otherwise) on South Korean soil that could not be better served by maintaining the status quo – as long as the US security commitment remains credible. As with Japan, US extended deterrence is key to ensuring that South Korea forgoes nuclear arms. Fortunately, at the time of writing, the US–ROK alliance has never been healthier.

Until North Korea carried out its first nuclear-weapons test, in 2006, it was frequently assessed that, if Pyongyang obtained such weapons, South Korea would feel obliged to follow suit. But a decade of subsequent nuclear tests, threats and conventional attacks has not provoked such a reaction. The popular mood in South Korea was supportive of domestic nuclear-weapons development even before Pyongyang conducted such tests. In any case, public opinion, while worrisome, is not in line with government policy, which is based on a more careful analysis of the pros and cons. Similarly, the unification of North and South Korea would almost certainly lead to the elimination of nuclear weapons from the peninsula. The scenario that would be most likely to spark Korean nuclearisation is that in which Japan pursues nuclear arms, triggering the much-discussed domino effect. For reasons explained in Chapter Two, such a development is unlikely to occur – although that conclusion also depends on the credibility of US extended deterrence.

Notes

1 Jiyoon Kim, 'The Fallout: South Korean Public Opinion Following North Korea's Third Nuclear Test', Asan Institute for Policy Studies, 24 February 2013, http://en.asaninst. org/contents/issue-brief-no-46-the-fallout-south-korean-public-opinion-following-north-koreas-third-nuclear-test/.

2 Jonathan D. Pollack and Mitchell B. Reiss, 'South Korea: The Tyranny of Geography and the Vexations of History', in Kurt Campbell et al. (eds), *The Nuclear Tipping Point: Why States Reconsider Their Nuclear Choices* (Washington DC: Brookings Institute, 2004), Chapter Ten, p. 262.

3 South Korea did not overtake the North in per capita output until the mid-1970s. During that decade, North Korean forces outnumbered the South's three to one, and the ROK did not yet have a qualitative edge.

4 The Guam Doctrine, or Nixon Doctrine as it is often called, affirmed that the US would supply arms but not military forces to its allies, who were expected to take primary responsibility for their defence.

5 Pollack and Reiss, 'South Korea', p. 261.

6 Seung-young Kim, 'Security, Nationalism and the Pursuit of Nuclear Weapons and Missiles: The South Korean Case, 1970–82', *Diplomacy and Statecraft*, vol. 12, no. 4, December 2001, p. 55; Peter Hayes, Moon Chung-in and Scott Bruce, 'Park Chung Hee, the US–ROK Strategic Relationship, and the Bomb', *Asia-Pacific Journal*, 31 October 2011, http://www.japanfocus.org/-Scott-Bruce/3630.

7 Selig Harrison, 'North Korea and the Future of East Asia Nuclear Stability', in N. S. Sisodia, V. Krishnappa and Priyanka Singh (eds), *Proliferation and Emerging Nuclear Order in the Twenty-First Century* (New Delhi: Academic Foundation, 2009), p. 54.

8 Peter Hayes, 'The Republic of Korea and the Nuclear Issue', in Andrew Mack (ed.), *Asian Flashpoints: Security and the Korean Peninsula* (Canberra: Allen and Unwin, 1993), Chapter Six, p. 52.

9 Kang Choi and Joon-sung Park, 'South Korea: Fears of Abandonment and Entrapment', in Muthiah Alagappa (ed.), *The Long Shadow: Nuclear Weapons and Security in 21st Century Asia* (Stanford, CA: Stanford University Press, 2008), Chapter 13, p. 399.

10 Taewoo Kim, 'South Korea's Nuclear Future: Temptation, Frustration and Vision', paper presented to the conference 'Over the Horizon: WMD Proliferation 2020', Center for Contemporary Conflict, Singapore, 12–13 September 2007, pp. 7–8.

11 Kim, 'Security, Nationalism and the Pursuit of Nuclear Weapons and Missiles', p. 69.

12 US Department of State, 'ROK Plans to Develop Nuclear Weapons and Missiles', 4 March 1975, available at http://digitalarchive.wilsoncenter.org/document/114616; US Embassy in Seoul, 'ROK Plans to Develop Nuclear Weapons and Missiles', 12 March 1975, available at http://digitalarchive.wilsoncenter.org/document/114615.

13 'Seoul Planned Nuclear Weapons until 1991', *Jane's Defence Weekly*, 2 April 1994, p. 6, cited in T.V. Paul, *Power versus Prudence: Why Nations Forgo Nuclear Weapons* (Montreal: McGill-Queen's University Press, 2000), p. 121.

14 Interview with Jo Dong-joon, August 2014. See Lee Eun Young, 'ADD mugigaebal 3chongsaui haegmisail gaebalbihwa (Oral Testimony from the Three Engineers for Weapons Development in ADD)', *ShinDongA*, December 2006, http://shindonga. donga.com/docs/magazine/shin/20 06/12/13/200612130500004/20061213 0500004_1.html.

15 Kori-1, a commercial nuclear reactor, began operation in 1978 and could have been used to produce weapons-grade plutonium, but this option was never explored, as far as is known.

16 Choi and Park, 'South Korea', p. 378.

17 Discussions in Seoul, July and November 2014.

18 Kim, 'Security, Nationalism and the Pursuit of Nuclear Weapons and Missiles', p. 60.

19 Hayes, Moon and Bruce, 'Park Chung Hee, the US–ROK Strategic Relationship, and the Bomb'.

20 Harrison, 'North Korea and the Future of East Asia Nuclear Stability', p. 56. See also Paul, *Power versus Prudence:* p. 121.

21 The statement is available in English at http://fas.org/news/ skorea/1991/911108-d4111.htm.

22 Brookings Institution, '50 Facts about Nuclear Weapons Today', 28 April 2014, http:// www.brookings.edu/research/ articles/2014/04/28-50-nuclear-facts.

23 Chung Won-shik and Yon Hyong-muk, 'Joint Declaration of South and North Korea on the Denuclearization of the Korean Peninsula', 19 February 1992, http://cns.miis.edu/ inventory/pdfs/aptkoreanuc.pdf.

24 Interviews with scholars and former officials in Seoul, July and August 2014.

25 See Kim, 'South Korea's Nuclear Future', pp. 12–13; and Harrison, 'North Korea and the Future of East Asia Nuclear Stability', pp. 56–7.

26 Kim, 'South Korea's Nuclear Future', pp. 17–18.

27 IAEA, 'Implementation of the NPT Safeguards Agreement in the Republic of Korea', 11 November 2004, paragraphs 12, 15, 22, 37.

28 *Ibid.*, paragraphs 27–34.

29 Pierre Goldschmidt, 'Exposing Nuclear Non-compliance', *Survival*, vol. 51, no. 1, February–March 2009, p. 153.

30 IAEA, 'IAEA Board Concludes Consideration of Safeguards in South Korea', 26 November 2004, http://www.iaea.org/NewsCenter/ News/2004/south_korea.html.

31 Interview in Seoul, July 2014.

32 IAEA, 'Safeguards Implementation Report for 2007', May 2008, paragraphs 34–5, http://www. iaea.org/safeguards/documents/ es2007.pdf. The broader conclusion under the Additional Protocol goes beyond the conclusions the IAEA is able to make under the comprehensive safeguards, which are limited to declared nuclear material and facilities.

33 Kim, 'South Korea's Nuclear Future', pp. 18–19.

34 Interviews in South Korea, August and October 2014.

35 World Nuclear Association, 'Nuclear Power in South Korea', updated October 2015, http://www.world-nuclear.org/info/Country-Profiles/Countries-O-S/South-Korea/.

36 Mok Yong Jae, 'South Overjoyed with Missile Victory', *Daily NK*, 8 October 2012, http://www.dailynk.com/english/read.php?cataId=nk00100&num=9890.

37 Jeffrey Lewis, 'Missiles Away!', *Foreign Policy*, 9 October 2012, http://foreignpolicy.com/2012/10/09/missiles-away/.

38 Daniel Pinkston, 'The New South Korean Missile Guidelines and Future Prospects for Regional Stability', International Crisis Group, 25 October 2012, http://blog.crisisgroup.org/asia/2012/10/25/the-new-south-korean-missile-guidelines-and-future-prospects-for-regional-stability/.

39 Jungmin Kang and Harold Feiveson, 'South Korea's Shifting and Controversial Interest in Spent Fuel Reprocessing', *Nonproliferation Review*, Spring 2001, p. 71.

40 Meeyoung Cho, 'As Nuclear Waste Piles Up, South Korea Faces Storage Crisis', *Scientific American*, 12 October 2014, cited in Toby Dalton and Alexandra Francis, 'South Korea's Search for Nuclear Sovereignty', National Bureau of Asian Research, *Asian Policy*, no. 19, January 2015, p. 123, http://nbr.org/publications/element.aspx?id=797.

41 Duyeon Kim, 'Beyond the Politics of the U.S.–South Korea 123 Agreement', Carnegie Endowment for International Peace, 29 October 2014, http://carnegieendowment.org/2014/10/29/beyond-politics-of-

u.s.-south-korea-123-agreement/ht20.

42 Under US law, advance consent is required to enrich or reprocess nuclear material that was supplied by the US or used in US-supplied reactors. Either condition makes it 'US-obligated'.

43 Dalton and Francis, 'South Korea's Search for Nuclear Sovereignty'.

44 Kim, 'South Korea's Nuclear Future', p. 37.

45 Discussions in London, September 2012, and Seoul, August 2014.

46 Interview in Washington, September 2014.

47 Discussion in Seoul, July 2014.

48 Chen Kane, Stephanie C. Lieggi and Miles A. Pomper, 'Time for Leadership: South Korea and Nuclear Nonproliferation', *Arms Control Today*, March 2011, https://www.armscontrol.org/print/4722.

49 Fred McGoldrick, 'The New Peaceful Nuclear Cooperation Agreement Between South Korea and the United States: From Dependence to Parity', Korea Economic Institute of America, September 2015, http://blog.keia.org/wp-content/uploads/2015/08/KEI_Special-Studies_Web-final.pdf.

50 Soo-Yeon Kim, 'New S. Korea–U.S. Nuke Deal to be "Win–Win" for Both: Einhorn', Yonhap, 19 March 2015, http://english.yonhapnews.co.kr/interview/2015/03/19/71/0800000000AEN20150319006700315F.html.

51 US General Accounting Office, 'Quick and Secret Construction of Plutonium Reprocessing Plants: A Way to Nuclear Weapons Proliferation?', 6 October 1978, http://archive.gao.gov/f0902c/

107377.pdf. See also Hayes, 'The Republic of Korea and the Nuclear Issue', p. 53.

52 Low burn-up spent fuel has a high percentage of the fissile isotope Pu-239, which is ideal for producing nuclear weapons. South Korea's four heavy-water reactors at Wolsong typically produce spent fuel with a plutonium mix of 66.6% Pu-239, 26.6% Pu-240 and 5.3% Pu-241, which is considered reactor-grade and suboptimal for use in weapons. The spent fuel would have a lower percentage of the Pu-240 isotope if it were extracted after a shorter than normal period of operation. See Charles D. Ferguson, 'How South Korea Could Acquire and Deploy Nuclear Weapons', Nonproliferation Policy Education Center, May 2015, pp. 11–12, http://npolicy.org/books/East_Asia/Ch4_Ferguson.pdf.

53 Young-sun Ha, 'Nuclearization of Small States and World Order', Asian Survey, no. 28, November 1978, pp. 1,137, 1,140. Ha did not spell out the factors that went into his four- to six-year timeline, other than to say that a separation plant could be built in a year or two.

54 James Clay Moltz, 'Future Nuclear Proliferation Scenarios in Northeast Asia', Nonproliferation Review, vol. 13, no. 3, November 2006, p. 595.

55 David Albright, Frans Berkhout and William Walker, Plutonium and Highly Enriched Uranium 1996: World Inventories, Capabilities and Policies (Oxford: Oxford University Press for SIPRI, 1997), p. 365.

56 Kane, Lieggi and Pomper, 'Time for Leadership'.

57 Kim, 'The Fallout'.

58 Cheon Seongwhun, 'South Korea's Responses to North Korea's Missile Launch', Center for Strategic and International Studies, 14 May 2012, http://csis.org/files/publication/120514_CheonPlatform.pdf.

59 64% according to Gallup Korea. '2/3 of S.Koreans Support Nuclear Armament', Chosun Ilbo, 21 February 2013, http://english.chosun.com/site/data/html_dir/2013/02/21/2013022100645.html. 62% according to Munhwa Ilbo poll, as cited in Toby Dalton and Alexandra Francis, 'South Korea's Search for Nuclear Sovereignty', National Bureau of Asian Research, Asia Policy, no. 19, January 2015, http://nbr.org/publications/element.aspx?id=797.

60 'South Korean Opinion Polls: Majority Favors Nuclear Weapons; 1980s Generation Questions U.S. Ties', WMD Insights, p. 2, http://cns.miis.edu/wmd_insights/WMDInsights_2006_01.pdf.

61 Norman D. Levin and Yong-Sup Han, 'The Shape of Korea's Future: South Korean Attitudes toward Unification and Long-Term Security Issues', RAND Corporation, 1999, p. 23, http://www.rand.org/pubs/monograph_reports/MR1092.html.

62 Seong-whun Cheon, 'A Tactical Step That Makes Sense for South Korea', Global Asia, vol. 7, no. 2, Summer 2012.

63 See, for example, comments by Yang Uk in Choi He-suk, 'S. Korea Cautions against Deployment of US Tactical Nukes', Jakarta Post, 14 May 2012.

64 The March 2011 opinion poll conducted by Realmeter and tv-N

found 72.5% support for South Korea developing its own nuclear weapons and 69.1% support for the reintroduction of American nuclear weapons. Cheon, 'South Korea's Responses to North Korea's Missile Launch'.

65 Josh Rogin, 'House Pushes Obama Administration to Consider Tactical Nukes in South Korea', *Foreign Policy*, 10 May 2012, http://foreignpolicy. com/2012/05/10/house-pushes-obama-administration-to-consider-tactical-nukes-in-south-korea/.

66 Interviews with scholars involved in the poll, March and May 2015. The poll results have not been made public.

67 Jonathan Pollack and Mitchell Reiss wrote in 2004: 'notably absent from the political right's views is any consideration of a renewed nuclear weapons option … If there are any advocates of a "Gaullist" position in the ROK, their voices are not heard, at least not at present.' Pollack and Reiss, 'South Korea', pp. 272–3.

68 Toby Dalton and Ho Jin-yoon, 'Reading into South Korea's Nuclear Debate', *Asia Times*, 21 March 2013, http://www.atimes. com/atimes/Korea/KOR-01-210313. html.

69 Former National Security Advisor Chun Yungwoo has said: 'when I meet with generals, most say they believe that to deter North Korea having our own nuclear weapons would help. When they hear me explain the consequences, however, they realize they hadn't thought it through.' Discussion with the author. See also Ralph Cossa, 'US Nuclear Weapons to South Korea?', 38 North, 13 July 2011, http://38north.org/2011/07/rcossa071211/.

70 'N. Korea Threatens to Turn S. Korea into "Sea of Fire" Over Leaflets', Yonhap, 14 August 2015, http://english.yonhapnews.co.kr/national/2015/08/14/37/0301000000 AEN20150814004900315F.html.

71 Jonathan D. Pollack, *No Exit: North Korea, Nuclear Weapons and International Security*, Adelphi 418–19 (Abingdon: Routledge for the IISS, 2010).

72 Kim, 'South Korea's Nuclear Future', pp. 26–7.

73 Interview with former senior official in Seoul, February 2015.

74 Joel S. Wit and Sun Young Ahn, 'North Korea's Nuclear Futures: Technology and Strategy', US–Korea Institute at SAIS, February 2015, http://38north. org/wp-content/uploads/2015/02/NKNF-NK-Nuclear-Futures-Wit-0215.pdf.

75 Jeremy Page and Jay Solomon, 'China Warns North Korean Threat is Rising', *Wall Street Journal*, 22 April 2015.

76 Kim Young-jin, 'Chung Calls for Nuke Redeployment', *Korea Times*, 11 May 2012.

77 Interview in Seoul, August 2014.

78 Comments by Lee Chun-geun of the Korea Economic Research Institute, cited in Dalton and Yoon, 'Reading into South Korea's Nuclear Debate'.

79 Hayes, Moon and Bruce, 'Park Chung Hee, the US–ROK Strategic Relationship, and the Bomb'.

80 Gerard Baker and Alistair Gale, 'South Korea President Warns on Nuclear Domino Effect', *Wall Street Journal*, 29 May 2014.

81 'Park Asks China to Help Dissuade N. Korea from Nuclear Test',

Yonhap, 23 April 2014, http://www.globalpost.com/dispatch/news/yonhap-news-agency/140423/park-asks-china-help-dissuade-n-korea-nuclear-test-0.

82 Choi Kang et al., 'South Korean Attitudes on the Korea–US Alliance and Northeast Asia', Asan Institute for Policy Studies, 24 April 2014, http://en.asaninst.org/contents/asan-report-south-korean-attitudes-on-the-korea-us-alliance-and-northeast-asia/.

83 Donald S. Zagoria, 'NCAFP Fact-Finding Mission to Seoul, Taipei, Beijing and Tokyo October 18 – November 2, 2014', National Committee on American Foreign Policy, November 2014, https://www.ncafp.org/ncafp/wp-content/uploads/2014/12/NCAFP-Asia-Trip-Report_November-2014.pdf.

84 Pollack and Reiss, 'South Korea', p. 267.

85 Christopher W. Hughes, 'North Korea's Nuclear Weapons: Implications for the Nuclear Ambitions of Japan, South Korea, and Taiwan', *Asia Policy*, no. 3, January 2007, p. 98.

86 Hayes, Moon and Bruce, 'Park Chung Hee, the US–ROK Strategic Relationship, and the Bomb'.

87 US Department of Defense, 'Press Briefing by Admiral Gortney in the Pentagon Briefing Room', 7 April 2015, http://www.defense.gov/Transcripts/Transcript.aspx?TranscriptID=5612.

88 Scott Snyder, 'South Korean Nuclear Decision Making', in William Potter and Gaukhar Mukhatzhanova (eds), *Forecasting Nuclear Proliferation in the 21st Century* (Stanford, CA: Stanford University Press, 2010), p. 171.

89 John S. Park, 'Nuclear Ambition and Tension on the Korean Peninsula', in Ashley J. Tellis et al. (eds), *Strategic Asia 2013–14: Asia in the Second Nuclear Age* (Washington DC: National Bureau of Asian Research, October 2013), p. 198.

90 Kim Taewoo, 'Role of Conventional Weapons & Missile Defense in East Asia: A South Korean Perspective', paper presented at the U.S.–Japan–ROK Dialogue on Nuclear Issues, Washington DC, 28 February–1 March, 2011, p. 3.

91 Scott Snyder, 'U.S. Rebalancing Strategy and South Korea's Middle Power Diplomacy', East Asia Institute, February 2015, http://www.eai.or.kr/data/bbs/eng_report/2015030618362920.pdf.

92 Interviews in Washington, March 2015. Richard Samuels and James L. Schoff, 'Japan's Nuclear Hedge: Beyond "Allergy" and Breakout', in Ashley J. Tellis et al. (eds), *Strategic Asia 2013–14: Asia in the Second Nuclear Age* (Washington DC: National Bureau of Asian Research, October 2013), p. 247.

93 Not all Koreans hold this view, of course. A senior government official and a leading academic in the nuclear field both said in October 2014 that the US security commitment is a more important variable than whether Japan were to go nuclear. Discussions with the author.

94 Peter Hayes and Chung-in Moon, 'Korea: Will South Korea's Non-Nuclear Strategy Defeat North Korea's Nuclear Break-out?', in George P. Shultz and James E. Goodby (eds), *The War That Must Never Be Fought: Dilemmas of Nuclear*

Deterrence (Stanford, CA: Hoover Institution Press, 2015), Chapter 13, p. 394.

95 Discussion in Seoul, July 2014.

96 Snyder, 'South Korean Nuclear Decision Making', p. 178.

97 Interview in Seoul, July 2014.

98 Quoted in John Lee, 'The Strategic Cost of South Korea's Japan Bashing', Hudson Institute, 5 November 2014, http://www.hudson.org/research/10775-the-strategic-cost-of-south-korea-s-japan-bashing.

99 The Genron NPO and East Asia Institute, 'The 2nd Joint Japan–South Korea Public Opinion Poll (2014) Analysis Report on Comparative Data', 16 July 2014, http://www.genron-npo.net/pdf/forum_1407_en.pdf.

100 Snyder, 'South Korean Nuclear Decision Making', pp. 178–9.

101 Kim Jiyoon et al., 'Challenges and Opportunities for Korea–Japan Relations in 2014', Asan Institute for Policy Studies, March 2014, http://en.asaninst.org/contents/challenges-and-opportunities-for-korea-japan-relations-in-2014/.

102 Kim Jiyoon et al., 'South Korean Attitudes on China', Asan Institute for Policy Studies, July 2014, http://en.asaninst.org/contents/south-korean-attitudes-on-china/.

103 Kim, 'Security, Nationalism and the Pursuit of Nuclear Weapons and Missiles', pp. 72–3.

104 Interview in Seoul, August 2014.

105 Address by President Park Geun-hye to the United Nations General Assembly, 24 September 2014, http://www.un.org/en/ga/69/meetings/gadebate/pdf/KR_en.pdf; remarks by Yun Byung-se, 'Journey to One Korea, One Korea Night', Davos, 22 January 2015, http://www.mofa.go.kr/webmodule/htsboard/template/read/engreadboard.jsp?typeID=12&boardid=14137&seqno=314816.

106 Pollack and Reiss, 'South Korea', pp. 282, 285.

107 The Rose of Sharon is the ROK national flower. On a similar theme, a 1999 action movie, *Yuryong* (*Phantom: The Submarine*) depicts threatened nuclear attacks against Japan by a renegade ROK nuclear submarine. See Kim, 'Security, Nationalism and the Pursuit of Nuclear Weapons and Missiles', p. 74.

108 Moltz, 'Future Nuclear Proliferation Scenarios in Northeast Asia', p. 600.

109 Mark Hibbs, 'Will South Korea Go Nuclear?', *Foreign Policy*, 15 March 2013, http://foreignpolicy.com/2013/03/15/will-south-korea-go-nuclear/.

110 Dianne E. Rennack, 'India and Pakistan: U.S. Economic Sanctions', Congressional Research Service, 3 February 2003, available at https://file.wikileaks.org/file/crs/RS20995.pdf.

111 Etel Soligen, *Nuclear Logics: Contrasting Paths in East Asia & the Middle East* (Princeton, NJ: Princeton University Press, 1997), pp. 82–99.

112 Elbridge Colby, 'Choose Geopolitics Over Nonproliferation', *National Interest*, 28 February 2014.

113 This view is voiced, for example, by Lee Choon-gun, head of the Korea Institute for Maritime Strategy, who points to the example of US acquiescence to Israel's nuclear programme. See Jihae Lee, 'A Case for the Development of Nuclear

Weapons in SK', *Daily NK*, 29 June 2015, http://www.dailynk.com/english/read.php?cataId=nko2501&num=13310. Pulling out of the NPT to overtly acquire nuclear weapons would be viewed as far worse than not joining the treaty and quietly going nuclear.

[114] Philip Iglauer, 'Nuclear Weapons for South Korea', *Diplomat*, 14 August 2014, http://thediplomat.com/2014/08/nuclear-weapons-for-south-korea/.

[115] Hyon-Sang Ahn, 'Will South Korea Develop Nuclear Weapons?', paper presented at the research seminar 'Nuclear Proliferation Trends and Trigger Events', James Martin Center for Non-Proliferation Studies, Monterey, CA, Spring 2010. Ahn, an ROK diplomat, wrote the paper in a personal capacity.

[116] Hayes, Moon and Bruce, 'Park Chung Hee, the US–ROK Strategic Relationship, and the Bomb'.

[117] Iglauer, 'Nuclear Weapons for South Korea'.

[118] Choi and Park, 'South Korea', Chapter 13, p. 395.

[119] Lee Chung Min, 'South Korea's Strategic Thinking on North Korea and Beyond', Asan Institute for Policy Studies, 7 October 2013, http://www.theasanforum.org/south-koreas-strategic-thinking-on-north-korea-and-beyond/.

CHAPTER TWO

Japan

For much of the past half-century, Japan has been considered to be a likely candidate for nuclear proliferation. It has both the means and the motive to do so. The nation's highly developed industrial base features advanced nuclear technologies, including those for both uranium enrichment and plutonium reprocessing. It has had contentious relations with nuclear-armed neighbours, first the Soviet Union, then China and now also North Korea. Yet for 50 years, constraints on nuclearisation have outweighed the motivations. An aversion to nuclear weapons in light of Hiroshima and Nagasaki remains strong among the citizenry and the scientific community, and this is reinforced by law and practice. Going nuclear would have prohibitively high opportunity costs in terms of commerce, diplomacy and national security. Every government examination of the nuclear question over the years has thus reached the same conclusion: it is wiser for Japan to rely for its ultimate security on the US alliance than to seek an indigenous nuclear deterrent. Yet Japan has in the meantime employed a quasi nuclear-hedging strategy that would enable a quick-start nuclear-weapons programme, should circumstances dramatically change for the worse. Ensuring that the country does not develop nuclear arms therefore depends to a great extent on the credibility of the US extended-deterrence commitment, which shows no sign of ebbing.

History

During the Second World War, the Japanese imperial army and navy pursued parallel nuclear-weapons programmes. The army's 'Project Ni' was based on the gas-diffusion method of uranium enrichment; the navy's 'Project F' focused on gas-centrifuge-enrichment technology. Impeded by material shortages and competing government priorities, neither project progressed beyond the laboratory stage, although Japanese scientists did learn how to trigger a fission reaction, and the amount of uranium required for a bomb.[1]

Japanese interest in nuclear weapons reawakened a decade later, encouraged by the US and France. The US Joint Chiefs of Staff considered in the late 1950s transferring nuclear weapons to the Japan Self-Defense Forces (JSDF), under a scheme similar to NATO's nuclear-sharing arrangements.[2] Prime minister Nobusuke Kishi, in office from 1957 to 1960, believed that Japan needed to possess nuclear weapons if it was to have global influence.[3] In the early 1960s, his successor, Hayato Ikeda, also expressed an interest in nuclear arms.

Nuclear weapons were introduced to US-occupied Okinawa in December 1954, amid a US–China crisis over the Taiwan Strait. By 1967 about 1,200 of the nuclear gravity bombs were deployed at Kadena Air Base, though they had been removed by the time that Okinawa reverted to Japanese control, in May 1972. The Pentagon also transferred non-nuclear components of such weapons to US bases in Japan itself, in the hope that complete weapons eventually could be deployed there.[4] Meanwhile, under a secret clause of the US–Japan Security

Treaty (see below), US bombers and warships transited Japan while carrying nuclear weapons.

China's nuclear test in October 1964 prompted prime minister Eisaku Sato to tell US ambassador to Japan Edwin Reischauer that Tokyo should have nuclear weapons too.[5] Follow-on discussions with US president Lyndon Johnson and the US secretary of defense Robert McNamara, suggest, however, that Sato's reference to nuclear weapons was a diplomatic ploy designed to strengthen Washington's deterrence promise – and, indeed, the promise was strengthened.[6]

Nuclear studies

In the late 1960s and early 1970s, amid a public debate sparked by China's nuclearisation and international negotiation of the 1968 Non-Proliferation Treaty (NPT), at least five different government-related studies assessed the pros and cons of developing nuclear weapons. They all concluded that the best option was continued reliance on US nuclear deterrence. In 1967–68, a quasi-private study group called Anzen Hoshou Chousa Kai (Research Commission on National Security) concluded that a plutonium-based bomb would be easier to produce than one using highly enriched uranium (HEU); that the nation's first nuclear-power reactor, at Tokai Village, could be used to produce 20 bombs' worth of weapons-grade plutonium per year from indigenous natural uranium; and that Japanese companies and research institutions possessed the bomb-making technologies necessary to the effort. The study argued against such a course due to the huge production costs it would entail and the negative impact it would have on Japan's diplomatic relations.[7]

A second study – initiated by the Cabinet Research Office in 1967 and sometimes called the 1968/1970 report because it was completed in two parts in those years – similarly concluded that nuclearisation was 'possible and rather easy', but not desirable. Developing a nuclear deterrent would be enormously costly and politically divisive. It would also spark regional suspicion and result in diplomatic isolation. Other risks included the geological dangers of conducting underground nuclear-explosion tests on a seismically active archipelago. Given the concentration of its population in a relatively small area, Japan would remain vulnerable to a first strike from China even if it acquired a small nuclear force. This was precisely the conclusion that Sato's government had hoped for from the study, as it countered arguments from domestic pro-nuclear advocates and helped allay foreign concerns that Japan might head down the path to a nuclear weapon.[8] A 1969 study by the National Institute for Defense Studies, under the Japan Defense Agency (JDA), reached similar conclusions.[9]

Complementing the main recommendation, the 1968/1970 report also advocated a nuclear-hedging strategy. It judged it 'vital' that Japan achieve a sufficient degree of nuclear independence, for both military and economic security. The authors thus recommended that Japan build gaseous-diffusion uranium-enrichment plants to reduce dependence on US-origin uranium.[10]

A fourth study – this one produced by the Ministry of Foreign Affairs' Foreign Policy Planning Committee, and thus more official than the others, but termed a 'research paper' rather than a statement of policy – similarly concluded in 1969 that Japan should maintain its non-nuclear stance for the time being, while maintaining the latent economic and technical ability to produce nuclear weapons if such action was warranted by international developments. Given the overlap between civilian and military uses of nuclear power, so the argument went, signing the NPT would not prevent Japan from having a nuclear option, which could be put into play in ten years' time. Summarising the study, one foreign-ministry official wrote, 'we will continue to use nuclear power for peaceful purposes, on the one hand. On the other, we should be in a position where we can continue to develop fast-breeder reactors and other relevant installations so as to make nuclear weapons instantly in case of need.'[11]

An official study commissioned in 1970 by director general of the JDA Yasuhiro Nakasone, and produced in 1972 as a White Paper, also concluded that nuclear-weapons development would be ineffective because of the cost – consuming 40% of the defence budget for five years – and the absence of a nuclear test site. Producing 'defensive' nuclear weapons would invite an adverse foreign reaction and risk triggering war, the White Paper concluded. Nakasone, who had earlier been drawn to the idea of indigenous nuclear weapons, thus developed second thoughts.[12]

Government-sponsored studies on the desirability of indigenous nuclear weapons were again undertaken in the 1990s when the end of the Cold War, North Korea's nuclear quest and China's military modernisation changed Japan's security environment for the worse. The most widely discussed report was commissioned by the JDA, apparently with the intention of proving the negative consequences of a nuclear option.[13] As with previous government reports, it concluded in 1995 that joining a nuclear arms race would be strategically unwise and hugely expensive. The report foresaw no possibility of a conflict with China that would involve nuclear weapons. Interestingly – and wrongly, as it turned out – the report also judged that it was unlikely the US would allow North Korea to become nuclear-armed.[14]

The most recent government study that has come to light about the feasibility of nuclearisation was written in 2006, entitled 'On Japan's Capability for the Domestic Production of Nuclear Weapons'. Commissioned by a senior government official, it concluded that Japan had the technical expertise and facilities to develop a small nuclear warhead and that the nation's M-V and H2-A rockets had potential intercontinental ballistic missile (ICBM) capabilities, but that developing a prototype weapon would take at least three to five years, cost ¥200–300 billion (US$1.75–2.5bn) and require hundreds of experts and engineers. The journalist who revealed the report assumes it was produced without the knowledge of government leaders by bureaucrats who wanted to be in a position to offer analysis in the event that they were asked about the nation's latent nuclear capability.[15]

The key takeaway here is that every time the government commissioned a study, the conclusions were the same: going nuclear was neither desirable nor necessary as long as Japan could rely on the US defence commitment. None of the internal assessments were undertaken in order to justify nuclear weapons or because government leaders doubted their non-proliferation course. The purpose, rather, was to take stock at times of a new security environment and, by quietly leaking the assessments, to reassure concerned neighbours and friends of Japan's steadfast non-nuclear-armed posture while also reminding them of Japan's nuclear potential. This typically served to encourage the US to reaffirm its extended-deterrence commitment. Meanwhile, a nuclear-hedging strategy was never questioned and was sometimes explicitly recommended.[16]

Policies

Japan has adopted various legal and political constraints on not acquiring nuclear weapons. The 'Basic Law on Atomic Energy', enacted in 1955, mandates that the research, development and utilisation of atomic energy must be limited to peaceful purposes. In June 2012, the national Diet (parliament) added a supplementary provision to the Basic Law to insert the words 'national security' as an aim of the safe use of nuclear energy. Critics claimed that this change allowed for nuclear technology to be used for military purposes.[17] The government and the lawmaker from the conservative Liberal Democratic Party (LDP) who initiated the change, which was done without any parliamentary debate, claimed the intention was to refer to nuclear security, including anti-terrorism.[18] If so, the wrong phrase was used.

Contrary to common wisdom, the legal restrictions do not include a constitutional prohibition of nuclear weapons. Article 9 of Japan's constitution renounces war as a 'sovereign right of the nation and the threat or use of force as means of settling international disputes'. After the Korean War, clause 2 of Article 9, which says 'land, sea, and air forces, as well as other war potential, will never be maintained' was interpreted to allow 'military capability that does not exceed the minimum necessary level for self-defence'. This enabled establishment of the JSDF. In 1957, Kishi stated that nuclear weapons were permissible under this interpretation, provided that they stayed within the scope of the 'minimum necessary level for self-defence'. In 1965, the Cabinet Legislative Bureau (CLB), a body in the executive branch that has de facto authority over constitutional interpretation, confirmed this interpretation. Five years later, the JDA formalised this in doctrine, saying that a small-yield nuclear weapon would be within the minimum force level required for self-defence. The interpretation was repeated in the Diet in 1978 and 1982 by the CLB and in 2006 by Prime Minister Shinzo Abe.[19]

Notwithstanding the constitutional allowance for nuclear weapons, since 1971 successive Japanese prime ministers have adhered to restrictive non-nuclear policies. The basis for the set of policies is the 'Three Non-Nuclear Principles' introduced by

Sato in December 1967, formalised by a Diet resolution in 1971, and confirmed by successive cabinets. They prohibit Japan from manufacturing, possessing or permitting the entry of nuclear weapons into the country, or its airspace or territorial waters. Although Diet resolutions are legally non-binding, the Three Non-Nuclear Principles are regarded by many Japanese as a morally binding norm.[20]

Soon after he introduced the Three Non-Nuclear Principles, Sato became concerned that pacifists were using them to weaken the US nuclear guarantee. He thus announced in the Diet in March 1968 a new nuclear-policy formulation called the 'Four Pillars Nuclear Policy' to: 1) limit the use of nuclear energy to peaceful purposes as regulated by the 1955 Atomic Energy Basic Law; 2) pursue global nuclear disarmament; 3) rely on US extended deterrence for protection against nuclear attack; and 4) support the Three Non-Nuclear Principles 'under the circumstances where Japan's national security is guaranteed by the other three policies'.

Sato's four pillars for the first time explicitly stated Japan's dependence on US extended deterrence. They also introduced a conditionality to the Three Non-Nuclear Principles, keeping the nuclear option open in the event that Japan's security was not guaranteed by US extended deterrence.[21]

In actuality, the Three Non-Nuclear Principles are two and a half in number. A secret agreement dating from the early 1960s, which came to light four decades later, allowed US warships carrying nuclear weapons to make calls in Japanese ports.[22] Sato originally planned on only the first two principles; the third principle, on the entry of nuclear weapons, was added under pressure from other cabinet and party members.[23] But tacit permission was given to the US Navy over the years to carry nuclear weapons while in port and in order to strengthen the US extended deterrence. The foreign minister's private advisory board in 2003 thus recommended formally redefining the policy as the '2 ½ non-nuclear principles'. No action was taken on this recommendation.[24] In March 2010, however, when asked in Diet debate what Japan would do if threatened with nuclear weapons, foreign minister Katsuya Okada from the leftist Democratic Party of Japan said 'if Japan's security cannot be protected without temporary calls by US vessels carrying nuclear weapons, the government would have to make a decision even if it has political consequences'. His words were common sense and simply expressed what has been de facto policy for many years. Nevertheless, it was interesting that Okada, who as noted below has strong disarmament inclinations, should have been the one to say it in the Diet, and thereby codify the policy.

Treaties and other international obligations

Although Japan today is a leading champion of the NPT, this was not always the case. It took Japan 18 months to sign the treaty after it was opened for signature on 1 July 1968, and another six years to ratify the NPT. The reasons for hesitation were mixed. Many Japanese resented the treaty's inequity between nuclear 'haves' and 'have-nots' and feared the former would never disarm. There was a concern that giving up a nuclear option would forever assign Japan to a second-class global status, while nuclear-armed states, particularly China, maintained power to exert their will. For reasons of national security, policymakers wanted to keep a nuclear-weapons option for the future. Senior Foreign Ministry officials told US counterparts that Japan might need to consider nuclear weapons if India or other non-NPT signatories became nuclear-armed or if China's nuclear threat were to increase.[25] There was also a strong commercial motivation not to be treated disadvantageously vis-à-vis Europe's nuclear industry in terms of international inspections and access to advanced nuclear technologies.

During negotiations on the treaty, the US assured both Japan and West Germany that Article IV would not interfere with dual-use civil nuclear programmes.[26] Allowances for reprocessing in particular were reaffirmed before Japan ratified the treaty. Upon signing the NPT in February 1970, Japan attached a statement reflecting its interpretation that the only proscribed nuclear activities were acquisition or control over nuclear weapons or explosive devices and that the pursuit of peaceful nuclear activities by non-nuclear weapons states could not be subject to discriminatory treatment, even if such activities could have a dual use in weapons development. The statement stipulated that the NPT should be the first step toward complete nuclear disarmament. The statement also reaffirmed Japan's right to withdraw from the treaty under Article X if the 'supreme interests of the nation' were endangered.

Despite the reassurances Japan received in connection with signing the NPT, it still took six years to develop a consensus on ratification, which raised doubts internationally about Japan's intentions. Indeed, some conservative forces within the governing LDP remained opposed because they wanted a nuclear option, while some leftist forces opposed ratification because the treaty allowed five states to remain nuclear-armed. Equal treatment with the European Atomic Energy Community (Euratom) was not assured until a safeguards agreement was negotiated with the International Atomic Energy Agency (IAEA) in 1975 and signed the next year. Lingering worries about the credibility of the US alliance in the aftermath of president Nixon's 1972 visit to China and the suspension of dollar–gold convertibility, neither with prior consultation, may have contributed to the delay.[27]

When the NPT came up for indefinite extension in 1995, there remained some hesitation in Japan on the grounds that the US nuclear umbrella could not always be relied upon and that an indigenous option therefore should not be given up forever. Under pressure from the US and other states, Japan supported indefinite extension, but referred publicly to the NPT withdrawal clause, as noted below.

Over the following years, Japan adopted other international instruments that strengthened its non-proliferation commitments. In 1996, Japan was among the first to sign the Comprehensive Nuclear Test-Ban Treaty (CTBT), which it ratified the next year. In 1999, Japan became the first country with a fully developed nuclear fuel cycle to have in place the Additional Protocol, the IAEA's strengthened safeguards system. Four and a half years later, the IAEA drew the 'broader conclusion' under the Additional Protocol that all nuclear material in the country remains in peaceful activities, a conclusion that has been reached every year since.

The IAEA keeps an office in Japan exclusively for safeguards in that country, which accounts for nearly 17% of the IAEA's safeguards budget – more than any other state. Further attesting to Japan's non-proliferation reputation, a Japanese citizen, Yukiya Amano, has headed the IAEA since 2009. Earlier, Japan was a founding member of the Zangger Committee (1971) and of the Nuclear Suppliers Group (1974), both of which seek to control the export of materials and equipment that could be applicable to the development of nuclear weapons.

Over the past three decades, Japan's international disarmament activism has generally increased. Since 1983, the Foreign Ministry has sponsored study visits to Hiroshima and Nagasaki through the United Nations Programme of Fellowships on Disarmament for diplomats from 150 countries. Annually since 1989, the ministry organises a UN Conference on Disarmament in a different Japanese city, with international experts. Japan financed a large percentage of the cost of the negotiations that led to the CTBT in 1998. It also funded negotiations for the Central Asian Nuclear-Weapons Free Zone.

Among the latest of Japan's disarmament initiatives was a 'Nuclear Disarmament and Non-proliferation Policy Speech' by Foreign Minister Fumio Kishida in January 2014 calling for nuclear-weapons states to reduce the role of nuclear weapons for consideration 'only in extreme circumstances based on the right of individual or collective self-defence'. Giving the speech in his home town of Nagasaki, Kishida naturally played up Japan's experience of being the only country to suffer the wartime use of nuclear weapons. Japan's emphasis on keeping alive the memory of Hiroshima and Nagasaki underscores its disarmament inclinations and contributes to the international disarmament movement.

At the same time that it promotes global nuclear disarmament, Japan relies on the US nuclear deterrent. As political scientist Nobumasa Akiyama puts it, the nation is 'caught between a moralistic view on nuclear weapons and the reality of today's security environment'.[28] The dichotomy often comes under the spotlight with regard to public statements. In 2009, for example, foreign minister Okada, who, as noted above, was the first to admit publicly that the Three Non-Nuclear Principles were not absolute, advocated that the US adopt a 'no first-use' policy with regard to nuclear weapons. The stance was opposed by bureaucrats who feared it would erode confidence in the US security guarantee.[29]

It was not surprising, therefore, that, in 2012, after the LDP had returned to power, the government declined to join an international statement declaring that nuclear weapons are inhumane and should not be used under any circumstances. Yet in 2013 Japan signed a similarly styled joint statement;

the incorporation of a few word changes to the text gave the government a fig leaf to justify the shift. At the same time, Japan signed a separate statement that noted the importance of recognising the security dimension, as well as the humanitarian concern, in the nuclear-weapons debate. Japan was the only country to sign both statements.[30]

The apparent contradiction of simultaneously promoting nuclear disarmament and nuclear deterrence might be seen to reflect psychological yin–yang impulses seeking both peace and protection. Japanese thinking on disarmament and deterrence has become more integrated, however. Today, both are rooted in fear of China. Promoting nuclear disarmament and transparency are tools for the Foreign Ministry to seek to contain China's nuclear build-up.[31]

Evolving defence policies

Many Koreans and Chinese believe that recent changes in Japan's defence policies could lead to a change in the non-nuclear stance as well. In recent years, Japan has shed most of the constraints that defined its defence policy for the majority of the Cold War era.[32] A prohibition on foreign deployment was lifted in 1992 to enable the JSDF to join a UN peacekeeping mission to Cambodia. Although JSDF peacekeeping forces have typically been deployed unarmed, in 2004–06 Japan sent an armed JSDF contingent to assist the US-led reconstruction of Iraq in a humanitarian role. A ban on power projection was effectively loosened in 2001 to procure in-flight refuelling tankers and later to produce helicopter destroyers, which are akin to aircraft carriers. And a ban on the military use of space was changed in 2008 to enable Japan to employ sophisticated military satellites.

In the defence development realm, a ban on joint military research was lifted in 2003 when Japan announced that it would explore the joint development of ballistic-missile defence with the US, and an arms export ban was lifted in 2014, when Japan announced it would supply missile interceptor parts to the US and the United Kingdom. Meanwhile, subordination of the defence establishment was changed in 2007 when the JDA was upgraded to a ministry.

A former South Korean ambassador to Japan, Kwon Chul-hyun, concluded in 2012 that Japan was 'getting rid of the obstacles one by one as the opportunity offers. In the long term, I guess it is preparing for a nuclear weapon.'[33]

All of these changes have made Japan more of a 'normal' military power commensurate with its leading economic status. The evolution has accelerated since Abe became prime minis-ter for the second time in December 2012. In particular, he has sought to push through the reinterpretation of the constitution to allow exercise of the right of collective self-defence if an ally is attacked. The reinterpretation, as decided ad referendum by the cabinet in July 2014, to allow use of force in defence of an ally is constrained by three conditions. There must be: 1) a clear danger to the Japanese people's right to 'life, liberty and happiness'; 2) no other appropriate means to repel an attack and ensure Japan's survival; and 3) a limit on the use of force to the minimum extent necessary. The reinterpretation was approved by the Diet in September 2015, but not without an intense political fight and more than 60% opposition in public opinion polls.

The nuclear taboo is of another order of magnitude and remains firm. As political scientist Etel Solingen notes, becoming 'normal' is not necessarily a prelude to becoming 'nuclear'; for the vast majority of states, 'normal' means being non-nuclear.[34] According to a close adviser to Abe, the prime minister has no interest in acquiring nuclear weapons.[35] Even if Abe wanted to, Japanese political and societal dynamics would constrain any such impulse, short of some catalysing event. As a group of leading American foreign-policy experts concluded after an October 2014 visit to Japan: 'the Japanese public and much of the ruling elite continue to be strongly unwilling to take risks or to significantly change a tradition of peaceful development and positive contributions to both the region and the international community that has become firmly rooted in Japan over the past 70 years.'[36]

Nuclear hedging

For much of the past half-century, Japan has had a quasi nuclear-hedging strategy, usually implicit in nature, which is the flip side of its posture of nuclear restraint. Some analysts disagree with the hedging interpretation. International relations scholar Jacques Hymans sees Japan's nuclear policy mix as the result of 'powerful forces of inertia', for example.[37] But many policymakers appear to quietly understand the hedging strategy. Japanese officials occasionally express it explicitly, with varying degrees of frankness and political acceptability.

As with Sato's 1964 comments about seeking nuclear parity with China, the hedging strategy is often seen as a means of diplomatic leverage. In an internal 1971 personal memo, Takuya Kubo, a senior JDA official, contended:

> If Japan prepares latent nuclear capability by which it would enable Japan to develop significant nuclear armament at any time … the United States would hope to sustain the Japan–US security system by providing a nuclear guarantee to Japan, because otherwise, the US would be afraid of a rapid deterioration of the stability in international relations triggered by nuclear proliferation.[38]

In his memoirs published in 1983, Kishi wrote in connection with a visit to the newly established Japan Atomic Energy Research Institute at Tokai in January 1958 that while Japan would concentrate on the peaceful uses of its nuclear technologies, 'as the level of our nuclear technologies increases for peaceful purposes, it will increase for military purposes, too'. He added that 'even without nuclear weapons, Japan would have a stronger say in the international arena – as in arms control and nuclear test-ban issues – by improving its nuclear latency potential'.[39]

At other times, hedging statements have more directly foreseen a potential need for nuclear weapons. In 1967, ambassador to the US Takeso Shimoda sparked a controversy by saying that, because the evolution of China's nuclear threat could not be predicted, 'the choice of whether or not Japan may become a nuclear weapon state should be left in the hands of Japan's future generation'.[40] The next year, agriculture and forestry minister Tadao Kuraishi had to resign for advocating an indigenous nuclear deterrent to protect Japanese fishermen from the perceived Soviet threat.[41] His was a unique case of a cabinet member calling for nuclear-weapons development, not just hedging.

In the past two decades, Japanese leaders have spoken more frequently about a nuclear capability. In July 1993, in the context of stating support for indefinite extension of the NPT, foreign minister Kabun Muto reminded Japanese reporters of the Article X withdrawal clause. He added: 'If North Korea develops nuclear weapons and that becomes a threat to Japan, first there is the nuclear umbrella of the US upon which we can rely. But if it comes down to a crunch, possessing the will that "we can do it" is important.'[42] In 1994, in response to a question in the Diet, prime minister Tsutomu Hata made an unprecedented statement to the effect that 'Japan has the capability to produce nuclear weapons'. Backtracking from what was said to be a 'slip of the tongue', the Foreign Ministry issued a statement saying 'mere possession of high-level nuclear technology and scientific technology does not signify the capability of producing nuclear weapons'. It then added: 'Japan does not have any expertise or experience in producing nuclear weapons. This means that Japan does not have the capability to produce them.'[43]

Four years later, former prime minister Morihiro Hosokawa referred to the latent capability when he wrote: 'It is in the interest of the United States, so long as it does not wish to see Japan withdraw from the NPT and develop its own nuclear deterrent, to maintain its alliance with Japan and continue to provide a nuclear umbrella.'[44] Hosokawa's statement reflects a consistent Japanese preference for relying on the US nuclear umbrella over indigenous nuclear development. It also repeated a consistent pattern of using the recessed nuclear capability as leverage to ensure the continued strength of the US commitment.[45]

Soon after Hosokawa's article was published, North Korea's test launch of a *Taepodong* missile that overflew Japan sparked a debate about nuclearisation in Japan. Prime Minister Keizo Obuchi reiterated the nation's non-nuclear weapons principles, but the next year right-wing parliamentary vice minister of defense Shingo Nishimura said in an interview that 'Japan may be better off if it armed itself with nuclear weapons' and that failure to do so left the nation vulnerable to international 'rape', comments for which he was dismissed.[46]

Comments about nuclear hedging accelerated in 2002. In April, leader of the opposition Liberal Party Ichiro Ozawa said he told Chinese leaders in Beijing that, 'if Japan desires, it can possess thousands of nuclear warheads. Japan has enough plutonium in use at its nuclear plants for three to four thousand. If that should happen, we wouldn't lose [to China] in terms of military strength.'[47] In May, chief cabinet secretary Yasuo Fukuda suggested that Japan might reconsider its decade-long commitment to the three nuclear principles if the international security environment changed dramatically for the worse.[48] In June, prime minister Junichiro Koizumi sought to close the issue by calling Fukuda's comments a 'slip of the tongue' and repeating the non-nuclear principles, but he added a hedging comment: 'it is significant that although we could have them, we don't.'[49] The next year both Fukuda and deputy chief cabinet secretary Shinzo Abe said that, while the cabinet had no intention of developing nuclear weapons at present, future makers of foreign policy should have the right to decide that question.[50]

Kyorin University professor Tadae Takubo and former Japanese ambassador to Poland, Nagao Hyodo, made the point more bluntly when they wrote that international politics was dominated by the principle of 'never say never' and that Japan should never say that it will never have nuclear weapons.[51]

North Korea's nuclear test in October 2006 ended Japan's taboo on discussing nuclear-weapons options. Foreign minister Taro Aso called for a public debate on the conditions that should trigger reconsideration of the non-nuclear policy. His main intent, however, was probably to elicit US confirmation of its extended-deterrence commitment, which indeed was dutifully repeated by secretary of state Condoleezza Rice in a visit to Tokyo that month.

In the wake of the Fukushima nuclear disaster in 2011, when many Japanese questioned the merits of nuclear power, former defence minister Shigeru Ishiba said 'We should keep [the] nuclear fuel cycle, which is backed by enrichment and reprocessing' in order to maintain 'technical deterrence'.[52] In two editorials, *Yomiuri Shimbun*, Japan's largest circulation newspaper, echoed Ishiba's call, saying that the nation's stockpile of plutonium 'functioned diplomatically as a potential nuclear deterrent'.[53] Before becoming defence minister in 2012, Satoshi Morimoto similarly said that commercial nuclear power reactors have 'very great defensive deterrent functions'.[54]

Such statements are sometimes referred to as a 'bomb in the basement' deterrence strategy, to keep potential adversaries such as China and North Korea guessing about Japan's capabilities.[55] As one Japanese defence official told this author, 'if China thinks the reprocessing is a deterrent, fine'.[56] The hedging strategy also requires maintenance of the capabilities. In 2014, a well-placed Japanese foreign-ministry official was reported to have informally asked US deputy secretary of energy Daniel Poneman to continue to allow Japan to reprocess plutonium because it was important for both energy security and national security. The official said US continued support for reprocessing was a fundamental of the US–Japan alliance.[57]

Capabilities

While the intentions behind Japan's nuclear-hedging strategy are often kept hidden, the capabilities are clearly visible. Japan has the largest number of civilian nuclear facilities of any non-weapons state and is the only one with complete fuel-cycle technologies, including both enrichment and reprocessing. A robust space launch programme adds a potential delivery capability to the nuclear latency. These capabilities are all dual-use; in the post-war period Japan has never been known to pursue any exclusively military-related nuclear technologies.[58] It has no known expertise in nuclear weaponisation or military involvement in nuclear technology. The transparency of the nuclear activities and the nation's unsullied record of cooperation with the IAEA provide confirmation that Japan does not have a nuclear weapons programme. The quasi hedging strategy only keeps options open for the future. Nuclear-policy expert James Acton calls this strategy 'existential hedging': maintaining a nuclear infrastructure without a deliberate policy to enable rapid proliferation.[59]

In this sense, nuclear hedging was a secondary rationale behind the nuclear capabilities. Energy security was the primary purpose.[60] For a country with no oil and limited coal reserves, nuclear energy was seized upon in the 1950s as a secure energy source. It was a far better means of seeking energy autonomy than the expansionist policies of the late 1930s and the disastrous war Japan began in 1941 to escape the Allied oil embargo.[61] The first nuclear power plant was built in Tokai in 1966, and before the Fukushima accident in 2011, 54 were operating. By 1998, nuclear power contributed 37% of the nation's electricity generation. This percentage fell to 29% in the following few years but was expected to increase to 40% or more by 2017. After Fukushima, however, all of Japan's nuclear reactors were shut down for safety checks. In mid-August 2015, just one was re-started. The cost of substituting more fossil fuel imports was US$156 million in the first three years after the accident.[62]

Closed fuel cycle

From the beginning in the mid-1950s, Japan's nuclear energy policy aimed to achieve a fully independent closed fuel cycle through recycling of spent fuel, in line with the practice of the US, its main technology supplier.[63] Japan saw the closed fuel cycle as a route toward energy self-sufficiency and as a hedge against global shortages of uranium, which in the early years of the nuclear age was wrongly assumed to be scarce. A more recent justification is to reduce the amount of spent fuel requiring disposal.

As a long-term goal, Japan aspires to develop fast-breeder reactors (FBR) that would produce more plutonium than consumed and thereby reduce uranium requirements by up to 60 times while also reducing nuclear waste.[64] As part of the research and development (R&D) programme to develop a commercial FBR, in the 1970s and 1980s small prototype reactors were built in Ibaraki prefecture (an area formerly called *Joyo*, after which the reactor was named) and Fukui prefecture (where the reactor was named *Monju*).

The FBR project experienced severe technical trouble, however, and, like fast-breeder aspirations in other countries, shows no prospect of ever becoming commercially viable. In 1995, a leak of the molten sodium that was used to cool the extremely hot reactor stopped operation of *Monju*, which has remained closed ever since due to safety concerns and a high-court ruling (molten sodium is a poisonous element that explodes upon contact with water.) Operations at *Joyo* were suspended in 2007 after an accident and have not yet been resumed. In 2014, the government decided to continue the fuel cycle programme but to use *Monju* as 'an international research centre for technological development, such as reducing the amount and toxic level of radioactive waste and technologies related to nuclear non-proliferation' rather than as a prototype for a commercial FBR.[65]

Meanwhile, Japan is proceeding with an interim plan, introduced in 1997, to recycle uranium and plutonium in spent fuel, involving separating it at reprocessing plants, and then mixing plutonium with uranium to produce mixed-oxide (MOX) fuel. This fuel would be burned in 16 to 18 specially designed power reactors, saving about half of the uranium that would otherwise be used.[66] The reprocessing project and MOX fuel plans have also run into major trouble, resulting in repeated delays and massive cost overruns.[67] Seemingly insolvable technological and political problems have also resulted in a huge stockpile of plutonium which, being weapons-usable, gives rise to proliferation concerns.

Uranium-enrichment technology provides Japan with a potential second path to a bomb. R&D on gas centrifuge uranium enrichment for civilian purposes began in 1979 at a demonstration plant in Ningyo-toge in Okayama prefecture. As with reprocessing, the purpose was to close the fuel cycle and thereby give Japan a degree of nuclear fuel independence. The first-generation industrial-sized enrichment was established in Rokkasho with a capacity of up to 1,050 ton-separative work units (SWU)/year. It operated between 1992 and 2010 but was never commercially viable as the centrifuges, with rotors made of maraging steel, repeatedly malfunctioned. A second enrichment plant using composite carbon-fibre rotors began operations at Rokkasho in 2011. The 1,500 ton-SWU capacity of the plant was to be sufficient for about one-third of Japan's pre-Fukushima low-enriched uranium (LEU) fuel requirements. The LEU produced there is not commercially competitive with prices on the international market. Yet the plant has been justified because it also has the purpose of further enriching the 700kg of 1.3% LEU that would otherwise be unused as a by-product of reprocessing.

US support for reprocessing

An experimental plutonium reprocessing plant was built at Tokai in 1975 and began operation in 1977. It has a capacity annually to process 210 tonnes of spent fuel and to produce about 450kg of separated plutonium. After the plant was finished at a cost of US$170m and 14 years of effort, a diplomatic issue threatened to prevent it from operating at all. In 1976 the US, which until then had promoted plutonium reprocessing for its recycling benefits, changed its policy. India's 1974 test of a nuclear device using plutonium produced and separated in ostensibly civilian facilities had shocked the US nuclear and foreign-policy communities. Plans by France and Germany to sell reprocessing technology to Argentina, Brazil, Pakistan, South Korea and Taiwan, all of whom were seen as potential proliferators, exacerbated concerns. With plutonium management becoming a political issue in the 1976 election, president Gerald Ford embargoed the export of reprocessing and enrichment technology and called on all states to accept a three-year moratorium on reprocessing. Jimmy Carter, who succeeded Ford in 1977, strengthened the policy shift, deferring domestic commercial reprocessing indefinitely and indicating that the US would seek to persuade other nations to follow suit.[68]

The policy shift came at an inopportune time for Japan, which was seeking consent to reprocess US-origin spent fuel at Tokai, and also permission to transfer excess spent fuel to the UK and France for reprocessing. When prime minister Takeo Fukuda raised the issue on a Washington visit, Carter handed him an internal report that recommended ceasing reprocessing. Carter's stance was seen as a threat to Japan's energy security and as a betrayal of America's previous encouragement of the nation's closed fuel cycle plans. According to Kumao Kaneko, a former Foreign Ministry official involved in the talks with the US, one reason Japan pressed for permission to reprocess plutonium was to ensure that Japan had a weapons option.[69] Japanese officials continued to lobby furiously and persuaded US Ambassador to Japan Mike Mansfield to weigh in personally with Carter to seek a compromise in order to preserve the health of the alliance. Gerard Smith, former director of the Arms Control and Disarmament Agency who was brought in to lead the negotiations with Japan, reminded Carter that threatening Japan's energy security in 1941 by cutting off its oil supplies had led to war.[70] It was also recalled that Japan was persuaded to sign the NPT only after its access to reprocessing was assured.

Carter relented and, after a study by the two countries of potentially more proliferation-resistant reprocessing did not yield any practical alternatives, he agreed to allow Tokai to reprocess spent fuel over which the US exercised residual control for two years and 99 tonnes per year. A two-year International Nuclear Fuel Cycle Evaluation study did not come up with good alternatives to conventional reprocessing, so Washington extended the agreement three times.[71]

When Ronald Reagan came to office, in 1981, he reversed US plutonium policy again, lifting Carter's ban on commercial reprocessing activities in the US. In order to keep Japan firmly in the anti-Communist camp, he also approved a new policy on foreign reprocessing of plutonium, subject to certain statutory conditions concerning safeguards and physical security. In 1982 the US and Japan began talks on negotiating a new nuclear cooperation agreement that was required in order to meet new conditions of the US Nuclear Non-Proliferation Act of 1978. The resulting agreement, which went into effect in 1988, proved to be advantageous to Japan by granting prior consent for reprocessing of all US-controlled (or 'obligated') material. Reagan's policy principle was that countries that had made huge investments in reprocessing facilities and had a sterling non-proliferation record were to be given advance consent.[72]

Permission was also granted to Japan to send spent fuel to France and the UK for reprocessing. Some of the recovered plutonium and uranium was eventually returned as MOX. In the absence of a functioning breeder reactor and the delay in operating of light-water reactors that could use MOX fuel, however, the plutonium oxide served no immediate purpose in Japan. More than 75% of the nation's separated plutonium remains in France and the UK, under contract to be returned by 2020.

When the Democratic Party recaptured the White House in 1993, Bill Clinton issued a policy statement that said: 'the

United States does not encourage the civil use of plutonium and, accordingly, does not itself engage in plutonium reprocessing for either nuclear power or nuclear explosive purposes. The United States, however, will maintain its existing commitments regarding the use of plutonium in civil nuclear programs in Western Europe and Japan.'[73] The Clinton administration concluded an agreement with Euratom in which the US gave prior consent to reprocessing along the same lines the Reagan administration had given Japan. These policies have remained in place since.

For both non-proliferation and nuclear security reasons, the US has encouraged Japan not to increase its large plutonium stockpile, which is also Japan's stated policy.[74] Washington has also persuaded Japan to return hundreds of kilograms of weapons-grade plutonium and highly enriched uranium that were transferred to Japan between 1957 and 1994 for civilian research applications under the Atoms for Peace programme, mostly for a Fast Critical Assembly (FCA). The UK also provided 200kg of 93% HEU for use at the FCA. Some of the HEU was returned to the US in small doses over the years. [75] The remaining amount, reportedly 214.5kg as well as 331kg of plutonium, is to be returned by the time of the 31 March–1 April 2016 Nuclear Security Summit in Washington.

The US–Japan nuclear cooperation agreement of 1988 comes up for renewal in 2018, although extension is automatic unless either side decides on termination. To protect against any US inclination to re-examine the conditions and change its policy, some Japanese nuclear bureaucrats argue internally that the government must have a solid plan by 2018 to reduce the plutonium stockpile.[76] One strategy favoured by many technocrats is to give development priority to 'fast reactors' that can consume large amounts of plutonium. Another option is to operate Rokkasho at a lower tempo than now planned.

Reprocessing plans

US policy under Reagan paved the way for operation of the much larger reprocessing facility under construction at Rokkasho since 1993 at a cost to date of US$22bn, three times the original estimate. It has the capacity to reprocess 800 tonnes of spent fuel annually, about 80% of the full amount of spent fuel from the 54 nuclear power plants that were operating before the Fukushima disaster. The fissile plutonium output would be 4.4 tonnes/year (or 8 tonnes of total plutonium). Rokkasho was to have begun operations in 1996, but has faced repeated delays due to technical, legal and political complications. Ongoing safety licensing procedures that were made more stringent after the Fukushima disaster have meant further delay. Meanwhile, it was decided in 2014 to permanently shut down the Tokai reprocessing plant, which had ceased operations in 2006.

Once Rokkasho begins operating, the operators plan to run it at a reduced tempo, to reprocess 880 tonnes of spent fuel in the first three years, producing about 4–5 tonnes of separated plutonium. In the same plant, the plutonium will be combined with uranium to produce MOX fuel. Doing this 'under a single roof' is a proliferation and security precaution in order to minimise the potential for diversion or theft of plutonium in transit between the processes.[77] The fuel fabrication is not expected to begin operation until 2018 at the earliest. If reprocessing starts before the MOX is fabricated and then irradiated, the stockpile of separated plutonium will increase.

Rokkasho was built in close consultation with the IAEA, so that the latest monitoring tools could be installed in the process line during construction.[78] Notwithstanding any hedging intentions, Rokkasho is obviously intended for non-military use for the present. As the largest facility ever placed under IAEA safeguards, however, Rokkasho will present safeguards challenges in terms of both cost – the US$10m annual safeguards bill will largely be borne by the Japanese government – and confidence in verification. As little as a 1% error in measurement of the plutonium would be equivalent to three bombs' worth.[79] The IAEA is thus readying a basket of verification techniques and technologies to supplement traditional measurement and accountancy methods.

Since 1991, Japan has had an official policy of no surplus plutonium. Any plutonium produced has to have a specific peaceful purpose. In practice, however, Japan has a huge surplus. As of the end of 2014, the plutonium stockpile amounted to 47.8 tonnes, 37 tonnes of which is held in France and the UK.[80] Technical delays in the breeder reactor programme and in developing MOX fuel meant that accumulated separated plutonium was justified as working stocks. The MOX fuel fabrication plant is now scheduled for completion in October 2017. In light of the uncertainties, a 'New Basic Energy Plan', announced in April 2014, repeated the no-surplus-plutonium policy but said the policy would be implemented with 'strategic flexibility'.

Use of the word 'strategic' in the plan had no connotation of national defence considerations but meant that the surplus will grow once Rokkasho comes online. Before the Fukushima disaster, plans called for 16–18 MOX-burning reactors collectively to consume about 5 tonnes of plutonium annually, which would have gradually reduced the stockpile. Operation of a new kind of reactor at Ohma would burn another 1.1 tonnes/year and *Monju* would consume 0.4 tonnes annually. But in light of more stringent safety requirements after Fukushima, less than half of the MOX reactors are expected to come back online. Utilities have applied to re-start seven of them, but even some of these face legal and political obstacles due to opposition by local governments that are alarmed by the negative

connotations of plutonium. New safety checks have also postponed the planned start-up of the Ohma reactor to around
2022, operation of which is also blocked by a lawsuit by the
Hakodate city government. As noted above, *Monju* will not
be used as part of the recycling programme. Masakatsu Ota,
an investigative journalist who specialises in nuclear matters,
judges that under the best scenario, only four MOX-burning
reactors will come online, consuming no more than 1.6 tonnes/
year of plutonium.[81] This is more pessimistic than most estimates, but it is very likely that operation of Rokkasho even at
a reduced tempo initially will produce more plutonium than is
consumed.

In addition to its inability to reduce the plutonium surplus,
the MOX reactor plan is beset by daunting problems. Japan's
MOX fuel costs up to nine times more than regular nuclear fuel.[82]
It would be far cheaper to dispose of the plutonium through
vitrification and burial.[83] For technical reasons, Rokkasho
cannot reprocess the spent fuel from MOX reactors, so an additional reprocessing plant would be needed, but currently there
is no realistic plan to build one. Separating plutonium for MOX
fuel also has inherent proliferation and security risks due to the
potential for diversion or theft during processing and storage,
even though the transportation risk is reduced by producing
MOX under the same roof.

Although long-term direct disposal of spent fuel is logi-
cally preferable to reprocessing, no local government in Japan
is willing to host a repository. Local politics is also a driver
behind the Rokkasho start-up plan. If the facility is terminated,
Rokkasho village and Aomori, the prefecture in which it is
located, threaten not to accept any more reprocessing waste
from France and the UK and to insist on removal of all the
spent fuel already stored there. In 2011–12, when the short-
lived Democratic Party-led government sought to end both

nuclear power and reprocessing, the Aomori governor essentially blackmailed the central government into continuing the reprocessing plan.[84]

Meanwhile, spent fuel is kept at fuel storage pools at Japan's reactors, some of which are close to full. Local governments of jurisdictions surrounding these reactors are reluctant to allow intermediate dry-cask storage, which can keep larger amounts of spent fuel securely stored for up to 100 years. Ideally, they should be persuaded to do so and Rokkasho operations postponed until there is a realistic plan to reduce the plutonium stockpile. Among the many experts who have studied this complex set of problems, the Princeton University-based International Panel on Fissile Materials in 2013 proposed a thoughtful road map on ways in which Japan could move out of its reprocessing trap.[85] Other experts have suggested that Japan should seek to persuade the UK and France to take ownership of the Japanese plutonium stored there,[86] that the law should be changed to regard the plutonium from spent fuel as a waste product rather than as an asset,[87] and that Japan should put excess plutonium under the custody of the IAEA.[88]

When the new nuclear energy policy was being formulated in spring 2014, some of those involved sought to include a corollary line that the government would take responsibility to reduce the plutonium stockpile. The timing was not propitious, however, because it would have appeared to be in response to criticism from China.[89] In February that year, the Chinese Foreign Ministry had seized upon what was intended to be a good-news story of Japan repatriating weapons-grade plutonium and HEU to the US to criticise Japan's plutonium stockpile.[90]

In light of the engineering and economic failure of Japan's closed fuel cycle, one Japanese policymaker told the current author that 'reprocessing is dead; the facilities are there but the policy is no longer possible'.[91] Although most Japanese bureaucrats, scientists and politicians associated with the nuclear programme strongly support reprocessing, some Japanese nuclear experts rue the decisions over the years to proceed down this path. In meetings with South Korean counterparts, they are known to recommend that Korea learns from Japan's mistake and does not pursue reprocessing. The remorse they feel is not held widely enough, however, for Japan to abandon the reprocessing programme.

If Japan were to abandon reprocessing, it would constitute a signal contribution to global non-proliferation. A group of distinguished US and Japanese non-proliferation experts recently concluded that Japan's policies have a significant international impact and that, consequently, Japan should give global non-proliferation factors more consideration in what to date has been a debate based on domestic matters.[92] A decision to give up the sunk costs of the Rokkasho reprocessing plant does not appear likely, however. The prevailing mood toward start-up of Rokkasho is 'business as usual'. This leads concerned foreign observers to ask if the reason is for a nuclear hedge.

Weapons usability of separated plutonium

The 11 tonnes of separated plutonium stored in Japan is theoretically enough for nearly 1,400 nuclear weapons based on the IAEA criterion of 8kg of plutonium needed to manufacture a nuclear weapon. The theoretical number is actually closer to 3,000, given that nuclear weapons can be made with as little as 4kg of plutonium each. In terms of technology, there is no doubt that reactor-grade plutonium can be used for nuclear weapons. The US proved this in 1962 with a successful nuclear test using reactor-grade plutonium.[93] The high level of radiation and heat emission from reactor-grade plutonium makes it dangerous to use, however, and the higher levels of the isotope Pu-240 can lead to pre-ignition and a resultant low yield. Reactor-grade plutonium has thus never been used for weapons.

Some might argue that the reactor-grade plutonium could be used in a crash programme if Japan were in a hurry to produce weapons. In particular, the spent fuel that is removed from the first reload of each reactor has much lower burn-up than the average and thus would be more suitable for weapons. It would be more rational, however, to use super-grade plutonium from the *Joyo* and *Monju* reactors. About 22kg of unseparated plutonium is available from production in the blankets in the *Joyo* reactor in 1977–78 and 62kg from *Monju*.[94] The purity is higher than weapons-grade. It is safeguarded and could not be diverted without the IAEA knowing. Additional weapons-grade plutonium could be produced by inserting a uranium blanket around the core of any other reactor or by simply operating light-water reactors for about 50 days. The low burn-up spent fuel thus produced could be separated in a small reprocessing plant that could be built relatively quickly given Japan's prior experience. A hot cell at Tokai could also be used for reprocessing, although its capacity is limited to about 2kg/year.[95] It is not likely that the Rokkasho reprocessing plant itself would be used, given its inappropriately large size, the need for remodelling if used for weapons purposes and because the facility would probably be deemed to be necessary for civilian reprocessing.

Rocket and other technologies

Japan's nuclear-hedging strategy is reinforced by space-launch-vehicle technologies that with further development could be applied to provide a delivery platform for a nuclear weapon. The three-stage solid-fuel M-V rocket that was developed in 1989 had a 1.8 tonne payload and a thrust on par with US intercontinental ballistic missiles.[96] When the programme was discontinued in 2006 on cost grounds, some conservative Diet members argued that it should be maintained for its potential military utility.[97] The M-V rockets were not designed for atmospheric re-entry, but re-entry technology has been developed since 1994 and was employed to bring the unmanned spacecraft *Hayabusa* back to earth in 2010. A controlled re-entry of the upper stage of a liquid-fuel H-IIB SLV was also successfully demonstrated in 2011.[98] In addition, with modifications the SM-3 Block IIA missile-defence interceptor that Japan is developing could be used to launch a medium-range ballistic missile.

There is no evidence to suggest that these technologies have been studied in Japan for ballistic missile applications.[99] The rocket designs are not well suited for effective use as ballistic missiles, being too large, for example, for use against nearby China and lacking necessary guidance control.[100] As the American authors of a seminal work on the subject put it in 2003, 'the contention that Japan's SLV program is a disguise for pursuit of a ballistic missile capability is simply absurd'.[101] Some Japanese do claim a hedging purpose, however. Lieutenant-General, Retd Toshiyuki Shikata, who worked as an adviser to the Tokyo Metropolitan Government in 2011, said *Hayabusa* 'sent a quiet message that Japan's ballistic missile capability is credible'.[102]

Even though the M-V has been discontinued for ten years, the space launch programme does provide the technological basis for developing a ballistic missile for military use. American defence policy expert James Schoff estimates that it could be done within two years.[103] In a 2009 study, Schoff noted several other nuclear-weapons-related technologies that have been perfected in Japan's industrial and research communities. These technologies include high-speed framing radiography, heavy-metal shock physics, explosive shaping and radiation hydrodynamics. These all contribute to Japan's nuclear latency. But Schoff found no indication of an orchestrated programme to develop these technologies as part of a purposeful hedging strategy and he noted that some key weapons technologies, such as metallurgical knowledge, were lacking. He also found that Japanese scientists were keen to demonstrate that they are not engaged in any questionable research and that a wide gulf existed between Japan's scientific research community and the defence establishment.[104]

Among other technologies necessary for a survivable nuclear deterrent, Japan lacks submarines that could be used to launch ballistic missiles. Given the nation's lack of geographic strategic depth, submarine-launched missiles are often deemed to be necessary to provide a second-strike capability. It also has been noted that Japan has no expertise in bomb and warhead design. These technical obstacles could all be surmountable, at least at the initial stage of nuclear deterrence. Rather than submarines, for example, Japan could mount nuclear-armed missiles on cruise ships, or take advantage of its mountainous terrain for tunnelling to hide missiles, as China has done.[105] The greater constraint might be political: summoning the collective national will to establish the legal, bureaucratic and political infrastructure necessary for a nuclear deterrent posture.

Break-out timelines

Among the 185 non-nuclear-weapons state parties to the NPT, Japan may have the shortest break-out time. Just how fast Japan could dash to build a bomb is a matter of considerable conjecture, much of it unsupported by factual analysis. Hyperbole is casually employed to suggest that Japan is just a 'screwdriver's turn' away from the bomb.[106] When he headed Russia's Foreign Intelligence Service in the early 1990s, Yevgeny Primakov said that Japan could make a nuclear device in five weeks.[107]

In Western circles, it is commonly suggested that Japan could produce a nuclear weapon in as little as six months.[108] American arms control expert Jeffrey Lewis assiduously sought to track down the derivation of the six-month claim and concluded that it is without technical basis. It appears to date from an offhand statement by a 'Japanese strategic thinker' in 1976 as cited in Richard Halloran's 1991 book, *Chrysanthemum and Sword Revisited: Is Japanese Militarism Resurgent?* Lewis quips that 'six months' is shorthand for meaning 'fairly soon', akin to the biblical phrase '40 days and 40 nights' as meaning a long time.[109]

The six-month common wisdom estimate based on a crude bomb contrasts with a Japanese internal study in 2006, which calculated that it would take at least three to five years before Japan could go into trial production of a miniaturised warhead.[110] Most US intelligence estimates have also been more cautious. A 1966 US National Intelligence Estimate concluded it would take approximately two years to produce and test a nuclear device, including the time needed to build a reprocessing plant and metal reduction facility.[111] A more extensive estimate the next year concluded that after the first device it would take three to five more years to develop a warhead compatible with a reengineered satellite launch vehicle.[112] One outlier to the cautious US intelligence community assessments was a 1999 report by the US Defense Intelligence Agency, which breezily concluded that 'Germany and Japan, which have developed their technology base and fissile material production base in support of their civilian nuclear power programs, could develop a nuclear warhead within a year should the political decision be made to pursue such a capability'.[113]

The Japanese and American government timeline estimates suggest a thorough, careful process in accord with Japan's usual way of tackling technological challenges. In a crisis mode, the

timeline for producing reliable nuclear weapons could probably be shortened to one or two years, especially if reliability
and accuracy were less important considerations. This is the
general assessment of American analysts who have studied the
issue with an eye to detail, although there is reasonable doubt
over timelines.[114] The need to develop a weapons design from
scratch – unless it could be obtained from an ally or via the
black market – could itself take a year or more if Japan sought
a sophisticated weapon on par with China's.[115] The technically
derived timelines are all artificial, however, because they do
not account for the legal and political obstacles that would
have to be overcome.[116]

If Japan were to seek to produce nuclear weapons, plutonium
is usually regarded as the most likely pathway. The possibility
of uranium enrichment must also be considered, however. It
might even be the preferred path if Japan were to seek nuclear
weapons quickly and did not need to miniaturise them. HEU
is easier to work with than high-burn-up plutonium and presents no radiation concern and less risk of pre-ignition. If stealth
were required, uranium could be obtained from an old unused
mine and small dedicated facilities for milling, conversion and
enrichment. Japan might also seek to produce HEU via laser
isotope separation, a technology with which Japanese nuclear
scientists experimented before 2001, when government funding
was cut. The equipment and know-how remain.[117]

Potential motivations

If Japan were to go nuclear, it would be the result of a severe
deterioration in its security situation in the face of a strong
threat and a perception that Japan could no longer count on
America's extended deterrence. A breakdown in the global
nuclear non-proliferation regime might add to the motivation.
Such a nightmare combination is unlikely in the foreseeable

future. And even if one or more of the factors did materialise, nuclearisation is far from inevitable.

In fact, each of these situations has arisen to a certain extent over the past two and a half decades. When the Soviet threat disappeared with the end of the Cold War, many Japanese worried that the US would have less reason to extend a defence commitment. China's nuclear modernisation and growing conventional capabilities threaten Japanese security, as does North Korea's nuclear posture. The emergence in Asia of three new declared nuclear states since 1998 showed an unravelling of the non-proliferation order. And yet Japan has steadfastly remained non-nuclear. It looks set to remain so.

Japan's continued non-nuclear status has belied many a prediction. In the late 1960s, Herman Kahn insisted that Japan would become a nuclear superpower within a decade and a half because it would not be able to sit by as neighbours acquired nuclear weapons. Zbigniew Brzezinski in 1972, John Mearsheimer in 1992, and Kenneth Waltz in 1993[118] were among the realism theorists who predicted that Japanese nuclearisation was a question of when, not if. This was also the view of the US intelligence community in 1957.[119] Many Japanese themselves in the 1960s thought so, too. In a 1969 Yomiuri poll, for example, 77% believed Japan would have nuclear weapons by 2000.[120] Yet it did not happen. Let us examine each of the potential motivations.

Korea

A 1995 report by what was then Japan's Defense Agency said that North Korean nuclearisation could cause Japan itself to consider going nuclear in the future.[121] Several foreign analysts made similar predictions.[122] Indeed, North Korea presents the most imminent threat.[123] Pyongyang's medium-range *Nodong* missiles presumably can carry nuclear and chemical weapons and can hit most of Japan.[124] A provocative article in the Democratic People's Republic of Korea (DPRK) state media in 2013 listed Japanese cities within range of the missiles. North Korea's 1998 test of an intermediate-range *Taepodong* missile that overflew northern Japan was a shock arguably comparable to the impact on America of the Soviet launching of *Sputnik* in 1957.[125] As noted above, the North's October 2006 nuclear test broke a public taboo on discussing a nuclear option for Japan.[126]

Yet what changed was merely the willingness to talk about the issue; only a small number of politicians on the far right actually called for Japan to go nuclear in response to the North Korean provocation. An Asahi public opinion poll after the test found that 82% of the Japanese population still wanted Japan to stick to the non-nuclear principles.[127] Having a nuclear neighbour was not new, given that Japan had peacefully coexisted with Soviet nuclear weapons since 1949 and with Chinese nuclear weapons since 1964. The lack of hysteria probably reflects confidence in the credibility of the US defence shield.[128] In addition, Japan has its own non-nuclear options for defending against nuclear-armed DPRK, including ballistic missile defence platforms and a potential to acquire pre-emptive strike capabilities.[129] For many Japanese, North Korea's failure to resolve the matter of Japanese citizens abducted in the 1970s and 1980s has been a higher priority than the nuclear threat.[130]

Strategic thinkers in Japan nevertheless remain concerned about North Korea's development programmes for intermediate and intercontinental ballistic missiles and, most recently, nuclear-armed submarines. A DPRK ability to strike the US mainland could call into question the credibility of the US deterrence. If North Koreans believed America might not be willing to risk San Francisco for Tokyo, they would feel freer to act aggressively toward Japan. As in the case of South Korea, this concern about decoupling complicates extended deterrence, although it should be noted that the US largely put this issue to rest in Europe during the Cold War with the Soviet Union.

Common wisdom in American security circles holds that if either Japan or South Korea went nuclear, the other would follow suit.[131] This is probably the case if Japan were to go first, for reasons cited in Chapter One. Yet the reverse does not hold, given the deeper anti-nuclear sentiment in Japan and the absence of any sense of a security threat emanating from the Republic of Korea (ROK). Japan's response to ROK nuclearisation would depend on whether the US defence commitment remained intact.

Yet Japanese do worry about the potential nuclear threat from a unified Korea. In the words of one former Japanese senior diplomat, a nuclear-armed unified Korea, combining the South's industrial capacity with the North's A-bomb technology, is the most realistic scenario that would spark Japanese nuclearisation.[132] At a recent seminar in Seoul, a Japanese scholar listed three troubling unification scenarios: the worst case for Japan is the emergence of a pro-China nuclear-armed unified Korea; the second worst is a non-aligned nuclear-armed unified Korea; the third worst is that North Korea's nuclear weapons go missing in a collapse and unification scenario.[133] Other scholars say that, even though the ROK government position is not to keep North Korea's nuclear arsenal under unification, the technology and know-how would be retained and perhaps the fissile material, as in the case of South Africa. Japanese also worry that some weapons and/or fissile material might be secretly kept.[134] US officials downplay this possibility, insisting that, in the event of North Korean collapse, the US would see to the thorough dismantlement of North Korea's nuclear weapons infrastructure and removal of its fissile material.[135]

China

While North Korea presents the most imminent threat, China is seen by Japan's policy community as the source of more serious and long-term danger. As noted above, China's 1964 nuclear test sparked overt discussion in Tokyo of seeking a nuclear equaliser. China's recent nuclear force modernisation has rekindled some of that psychological and strategic shock. China is seen as much more likely than North Korea to force US–Japanese nuclear decoupling.

Japan worries that the reality of mutual vulnerability between China and the US will be treated by Beijing as equivalent to Cold War-style mutual assured destruction that gives it freedom to assert itself at the conventional level. Speaking at a conference in Washington in March 2015, Sugio Takahashi from Japan's National Institute for Defense Studies said: 'If there is a mutual vulnerability at the strategic level between US and China, then conventional balance at the regional level matters, and Japan has a disadvantage because of lack of geographic depth. So Japan is concerned about the US accepting mutual vulnerability. China's nuclear policy aims to separate the nuclear from the conventional domain.'[136] Some Japanese worry that cuts in the US nuclear force could tempt China to seek to build up to nuclear parity,[137] even though the disparity in warheads today is in the order of 30:1 and China's nuclear posture is not based on keeping up with the nuclear superpowers.

Japan's sense of vulnerability vis-à-vis China relates in greater part to Beijing's growing conventional capabilities, economic rise, defence budget increases and assertive behaviour. China's increasing anti-access/area-denial (A2AD) capabilities, including the DF-21 and DF-26 'carrier killer' missiles under development, are seen as undermining US deterrence, even if they do not have the precision and lethality sometimes attributed to them.[138] There is a concern that China may be able over time to neutralise the naval and air superiority that the US and Japan have enjoyed in the western Pacific. A2AD capabilities that limit America's ability to project power in the region could undermine faith in America's ability to help defend Japan. Some Japanese security thinkers say that if China's conventional capabilities prevail, Japan may have to consider a nuclear dimension of its own.[139]

US commitment

The single-most important variable affecting Japan's continued non-nuclear posture is the credibility of the US extended deterrence. Credibility is a highly subjective criterion, depending on perceptions more than reality. Over the years, US credibility in the eyes of some Japanese variously has been threatened by US loss in Vietnam, force reductions in the region, the Guam Doctrine, withdrawal from the Philippines, inability to prevent China from becoming nuclear-armed and failure to stop North Korea's nuclear programme. Polls in 1969, 1971 and 1996 found that fewer than half of Japanese respondents believed the US would come to Japan's defence if it were exposed to extreme danger.[140] Most recently, the credibility of the nuclear umbrella has come under question due to US defence budget austerity, a reduced emphasis on nuclear deterrence, the failure to stop Russian aggression in Ukraine and Obama's decision not to employ military force against Syria after it ignored his red line on chemical weapons use.

Japanese strategists understand that the Ukraine and Syria cases did not involve US security commitments. More analogous to Japan's situation would be US failure to come to the assistance of a defence partner, such as if China threatened Taiwan. The concerning scenario need not involve conflict. If Washington were to cut Taiwan adrift in deference to greater

US national interests, as some American pundits have argued (see Chapter Three), it would give the Japanese reason to question the durability of the US commitment in their own case. The fact that the US does not have a treaty commitment to defend Taiwan, as distinct from the commitment to Japan, would probably be lost in terms of perceptions. China's ever-growing dominance as a US trade partner[141] already gives rise to nightmares in Japan that the US might someday choose China over Japan.

Some Japanese security specialists also worry about a reduced role of nuclear weapons in the US deterrence commitment. They want an 'unshakeable nuclear umbrella', as Abe put it to Obama in 2013.[142] During the 2008 US presidential elections, the Foreign Ministry sent senior officials to both the Democratic and Republican party campaigns asking that the candidates not offer to cut deployable nuclear arms to below 1,000.[143] Obama's subsequent New START Treaty agreed to cut only to 1,550 by 2018. But his commitment to a nuclear-free world in his 5 April 2009 speech in Prague exacerbated Japan's nuclear policy ambivalence. On the one hand, most Japanese citizens identified with the disarmament vision; yet Obama's emphasis on reducing the salience of nuclear weapons made policymakers nervous about the strength of the nuclear umbrella. In drafting the 2010 Nuclear Posture Review (NPR), US officials took Japan's concerns into account and rejected language that would have said the 'sole purpose' of the US nuclear arsenal is to deter nuclear attack on the US and its allies. Instead, the review maintained the role of nuclear weapons in deterring attacks by non-nuclear means that threaten vital national interests.

In the run-up to the NPR, Washington-based Japanese diplomats were reported to have argued semi-publicly that the US should not retire the nuclear-armed, submarine-launched

Tomahawk Land Attack Missile (TLAM-N). Foreign minister Okada sent a letter on 24 December 2009 to the US secretaries of state and defense denying that this was Japanese government policy and emphasising his own views in favour of nuclear disarmament.[144] The controversial Christmas Eve letter was widely criticised by LDP politicians and the security establishment, who claimed it undermined Japan's national security. They asked what would take the place of TLAM-N at the lower rung of deterrence in the deterrence escalation ladder. The US carefully considered these views and before formally retiring the missiles in question, and as a substitute, committed to modernising globally deployable nuclear-equipped bombers.[145] According to Japanese defence policy scholar Michito Tsuruoka, 'There is a strong consensus in Tokyo that it was well informed and adequately consulted regarding the NPR … As a result of this, Tokyo's concerns regarding the United States' nuclear posture, not least its adverse implications for extended deterrence, have almost disappeared.'[146] Sending nuclear-capable B-52 bombers and B-2 stealth fighter-bombers over the Korean Peninsula in March 2013 was additionally reassuring to Japan, just as it was to South Korea.

The fact that US Navy surface ships and attack submarines have not carried nuclear weapons since president George H.W. Bush's Nuclear Initiative in 1991 made the TLAM-N controversy surreal. Given the taboo against nuclear weapons use and the increasing accuracy and destructive power of conventional weapons, successive US administrations have realised that deterrence via conventional weapons is more realistic and credible than via nuclear weapons.[147] US operational capabilities and the will to use them in defence of Japan are the important criteria. This is why Japan worries about China's growing A2AD capabilities and assertiveness. America's apparent acquiescence to China's demand that the US and the

ROK not conduct a joint naval exercise in the Yellow Sea after the North Korean fatal sinking of the *Cheonan* corvette in March 2010 was a case in point.[148]

Japan is also concerned about China's 'grey-zone' provocations that are 'neither pure peacetime nor contingencies over territorial sovereignty and interest', in the words of one Japanese strategist,[149] such as regularly sending coastguard vessels to transgress Japan's territorial waters around the Senkaku/Diaoyu islands. To make the point that this is a matter for extended deterrence, updated guidelines for bilateral defence cooperation issued in April 2015 emphasise 'seamless, robust, flexible, and effective bilateral responses'.[150] To the Japanese, this means that the US could be involved from day one of a grey-zone situation.[151]

Obama's statement while visiting Japan in May 2014 that Article V of the US–Japan Security Treaty applied to the Senkakus because they are under Japan's administration provided helpful reassurance and went beyond what some observers had expected in light of the US refusal to opine on the final sovereignty on the Senkakus.[152] Some analysts thought Obama backtracked when he said at a follow-on press conference that this commitment did not mean the US would engage militarily every time international law was violated.[153] Abe himself has made clear, however, that Japan has primary responsibility to defend the Senkakus.[154] Obama's Asia-Pacific 'pivot' or 'rebalancing' strategy has also helped to reassure Japan about commitment and staying power. The number of US troops stationed in Japan – 54,500 as of 2015, including naval forces – may decrease by 9,000 under one Okinawa Marine redeployment plan, but the US military presence shows no sign of fading.

In response to China's A2AD challenges, the US Department of Defense developed the concept of 'Air–Sea battle', now labelled Joint Concept for Access and Maneuver in the Global Commons, which would entail strikes on the Chinese mainland early in a conflict to eliminate China's 'kill chain' of radars, command-and-control centres, and missile sites. Although the concept is controversial because of its escalatory potential, it helps to signal to both allies and potential adversaries that America's extended deterrence will not be undermined.[155]

Another way in which Washington has addressed Japanese deterrence concerns is by institutionalising dialogue on deterrence strategy and operations. Following up on useful consultations prior to US release of the NPR in 2010, the US and Japan that year established an Extended Deterrence Dialogue, similar to one the US also began with South Korea. According to Japanese officials, it has significantly contributed to sustaining confidence in the credibility of the deterrence.[156]

US abandonment of Japan is unthinkable under current circumstances. The US–Japan alliance is as healthy as ever and is seen by the large majority of the Japanese public and policy community as central to Japanese security policy.[157] According to polling, the credibility of the defence commitment is stronger than it was during the Cold War.[158] In 2015, 75% of Japanese said they trust the US.[159]

A strong alliance relationship is consistent with a different kind of nuclear-acquisition scenario for Japan: one followed in conjunction with the US. Most of the Japanese advocates for nuclearisation see it as a complement to US deterrence, not as a unilateral move in opposition to the US.[160] Samuels and Schoff outline three models for how this might work: 1) purchase or lease of US nuclear weapons with cruise missiles, with the US maintaining a right of launch refusal; 2) lease of US *Trident* missiles with co-development of a submarine platform and cooperation on warhead design, similar to the UK deterrent model; or 3) deployment of US nuclear weapons on Japanese territory under US control with release to Japan in the event of a crisis, similar to the NATO model.[161] The first two models, and arguably the third as well, would put both countries in violation of the NPT, as well as the Missile Technology Control Regime. All three models are only possible in the event of an irreparable breakdown in US–China relations and US willingness also to allow South Korea some degree of nuclear acquisition. However, the fact that several responsible Japanese strategists envision some form of nuclear sharing with the US means that it is not inconceivable.

Constraints

That Japan has remained a non-nuclear-weapons state throughout the post-war period, despite having both the capabilities and the presumptive motivations, points to the strength of the enduring constraints. The reasons Japan did not seek nuclear weapons at any time over the past 50 years remain dispositive today. As every internal study over the years has found, the social, political, economic and strategic factors all continue to weigh heavily against nuclearisation. Citing these reasons, former US State Department Japan expert Kevin Maher said in 2011: 'We've never had any concern about the Japanese government building a nuclear weapon.'[162]

Societal opposition

Seventy years after the Hiroshima and Nagasaki atomic attacks, an aversion to nuclear weapons remains embedded in Japanese culture and society.[163] Right-wing figures, such as former Tokyo governor Shintaro Ishihara, who advocate developing nuclear weapons remain on the fringes of the political spectrum. In spring 2013, after North Korea's third nuclear test and a string of provocative verbal threats, a public opinion poll by the conservative Fuji TV found 24% in favour of having nuclear weapons and 73% against.[164]

The disparaging term 'nuclear allergy' was first used by US secretary of state John Foster Dulles in 1954 to describe the anti-nuclear protests fanned that year by the exposure of a Japanese fishing crew on the *Fukuryu Maru* to deadly radiation from a US thermonuclear test on Bikini Atoll, an event that inspired the Godzilla film series.[165] In the years since, the 'allergy' has become part of Japan's DNA. Although the internal taboo against discussing nuclearisation has dissipated this century, the public reaction remains strongly negative against those who advocate nuclear weapons. Nuclear latency and hedging is socially acceptable but calling for exercising this option is not.

Adding to the moral arguments against nuclear weapons is the post-Fukushima mood against nuclear energy. In the words of former leading diplomat Yukio Satoh, 'the disaster made the Japanese public, housewives in particular, opposed to all things nuclear.'[166] He called it an exaggeration for the Atlantic Council to suggest that there is an ongoing debate in Japan about nuclear weapons,[167] which is promoted only by a small minority. The debate, rather, is about whether to continue nuclear energy at all.

Societal opposition to nuclear weapons is particularly strong in the academic and scientific communities, including in the nuclear technology field, which is both pacifist and leak-prone. If a hawkish prime minister were to decide nuclear weapons must be built, former Foreign Ministry official Kaneko believes that scientists and engineers would refuse to go along and that some would become whistleblowers. The openness of Japanese society is the most effective brake on a nuclear-weapons programme, he contends.[168] Hymans calls such pacifist scientists and other opponents of nuclearisation 'veto players', and notes that Japan has them in even greater numbers after Fukushima.[169] This societal transparency, combined with the highly intrusive IAEA monitoring presence in Japan, would make it nigh on impossible for Japan to pursue a clandestine path to nuclear weapons.

Economic and geographic constraints

The economic disincentives for South Korea to go nuclear apply to Japan as well. Bilateral nuclear cooperation agreements with Australia, Canada, France, the UK and the US all have stringent non-proliferation conditions, requiring return of all imported materials and equipment if the civilian nuclear programme is misused for military purposes. The leverage of this conditionality will be reduced if the post-Fukushima anti-nuclear mood and stricter safety measures keep most of Japan's nuclear power plants from resuming operation anyway. But unless Japan goes entirely nuclear-free, or finds the magic grail of a self-perpetuating closed fuel cycle, the threat of a nuclear supply cut-off is still a significant deterrent.

A decision to violate the NPT would also have an economic cost in terms of lost trade due to sanctions that would be likely to be imposed. Japan's lower dependency on foreign trade (33% of GDP for Japan, compared to 78% for Korea in 2014[170]) again means that this deterrent is less than in the Korean case, but it remains a non-trivial factor. In repudiation of the prior militarist model, Japan's entire post-war development has been based on the 'Yoshida doctrine' (after the first post-war prime minister, Shigeru Yoshida), emphasising the primacy of economic growth and reliance on the US for security. Deviating from this path and incurring both the economic costs of acquiring a nuclear deterrent and the various opportunity costs and indirect costs that this would entail would not happen without a sharp change to the Japanese psyche.

All of the Japanese government-inspired studies about the feasibility of indigenous nuclear weapons fastened upon the constraints imposed by geography. Japan's narrow area and concentrated population make it vulnerable to a first strike were it to enter into a nuclear competition with land-rich adversaries such as China or Russia. It may believe it would thus need a survivable second-strike capability by developing nuclear-armed submarines, as both the UK and Israel, states with similar geographic constraints, have done. In Japan's case, developing survivable submarines would take perhaps ten years. The nation's existing submarines have no missile launch capacity and are run by diesel engines, with attendant problems of noise and limited patrolling times. During the development phase for nuclear-powered and -armed submarines, Japan would be vulnerable to a pre-emptive strike. Other geographic constraints include the lack of an unpopulated space for nuclear testing and of a location for secure storage and deployment of nuclear weapons and delivery systems.[171]

Security considerations

An indigenous nuclear programme would fan an arms race and thus diminish rather than strengthen Japan's security. It would be intensely provocative to China, possibly sparking a further acceleration in its nuclear and conventional military build-up. Russia may also respond accordingly. Pursuing nuclear weapons might also increase the danger of a pre-emptive nuclear strike from North Korea. In addition, Japanese nuclearisation would provoke South Korea to seek its own nuclear arsenal, adding to regional tension and instability. A departure from the NPT of the most stalwart non-proliferation advocate would spell the demise of the treaty and the end of prospects for a nuclear-weapons-free world. A breakdown of the NPT would increase the chances of states in other regions also seeking nuclear weapons or at least hedging capabilities, almost all of which would be detrimental to Japan's security and trade interests.

On top of exacerbating security challenges from China, Russia and the Korean Peninsula, Japanese pursuit of nuclear weapons could lead to abandonment by the US or worse. Ishiba, the outspoken advocate of nuclear hedging, cautions against actual nuclearisation for this reason: 'if we develop nuclear weapons, that would be tantamount to saying we don't trust the nuclear deterrence of the United States ... we thereby could make enemies out of both the US and China, which is the scariest scenario.'[172]

National security scholar and former US Defense Department senior official Brad Roberts also puts the danger starkly: 'Japan's decision to seek an independent nuclear deterrent would presumably reflect profound lack of confidence in U.S. credibility; it is difficult to see how or why the U.S.–Japan alliance would survive a Japanese decision to acquire nuclear weapons.'[173] Roberts's view reflects the dominant thinking among America-based analysts.[174] Not everyone agrees, of course. Security policy analyst Elbridge Colby argues that circumstances would determine whether the US would give greater weight to non-proliferation over geostrategic considerations vis-à-vis rising China in responding to Japan acquiring nuclear weapons.[175]

An assessment that Japanese proliferation may be acceptable risks becoming a self-fulfilling prophecy. In early 2003, vice president Dick Cheney and Senator John McCain both commented that North Korea's nuclear quest might force Japan to seek a nuclear option of its own. Influential conservative columnist Charles Krauthammer wrote that the US should endorse a Japanese nuclear deterrent if China did not pressure Pyongyang into stopping its nuclear programme.[176]

Three years later, a former speechwriter for president George W. Bush similarly advocated exploiting the 'Japan nuclear card' vis-à-vis China and North Korea.[177] Japanese advocates of nuclearisation took such comments as an endorsement of their view. Japanese nuclear expert Katsuhisa Furukawa assesses that 'Washington's tacit or open approval' would be the most significant factor in fostering a Japanese decision to develop a nuclear capability.[178] Strategists Kurt Campbell and Tsuyoshi Sunohara thus argue that, however tempting it is to play the Japan card, 'American leaders and influential commentators both within and outside the government should never signal to the Japanese, even inadvertently, that they actually favor Japan's acquisition of nuclear weapons.'[179]

Assessment

Japan did not seek its own nuclear deterrent after China's 1964 nuclear test, nor after North Korea's 2006 test. Each time it had a better security option via US deterrence. It is thus logical to predict that any further deterioration in Japan's security environment would not spark a nuclear pursuit either, unless Japan had serious doubts about alliance credibility. Given the Asia policy focus of successive US administrations and the multiple forums for deterrence consultations, there is no reason for Japan today to harbour any such doubts. Should any doubts arise, Tokyo could be expected again to first employ a hedging strategy to encourage Washington to recommit.

This hedging strategy should be seen for what it is: a means of diplomatic leverage to ensure a continued American presence in East Asia and a way to keep options alive for the future should circumstances dramatically change. Meanwhile, although the option is being maintained by means of both the enrichment and reprocessing programmes, no visible steps have been taken to enhance the option or to shorten the timeline. One can instead see policy decisions in the opposite direction, including the discontinuation of the M-V solid-fuel rocket programme and the return to the US of weapons-grade fissile material. In the foreseeable future, the only way that nuclear weapons might appear in Japan would be temporarily aboard US ships or aircraft in the event that the government were to amend the Three Non-Nuclear Principles.

Notes

1   Katsuhisa Furukawa, 'Japan's Policy and Views on Nuclear Weapon: A Historical Perspective', *Jebat: Malaysian Journal of History, Politics, & Strategic Studies*, vol. 37, 2010, pp. 1–2. Claims that Japan developed and tested an atomic bomb in its Korean colony are without merit. See Walter E. Grunden, 'Hungnam and the Japanese Atomic Bomb: Recent Historiography of a Postwar Myth', *Intelligence and National Security*, vol. 13, no. 2, 1998.

2   Masakatsu Ota, 'U.S. Weighed Giving Japan Nuclear Weapons in 1950s', *Japan Times*, 23 January 2015.

3   Richard Samuels and James L. Schoff, 'Japan's Nuclear Hedge: Beyond "Allergy" and Breakout', in Ashley J. Tellis, Abraham M. Denark and Travis Tanner (eds), *Strategic Asia 2013–14: Asia in the Second Nuclear Age* (Washington DC: National Bureau of Asian Research, October 2013), p. 237.

4   Robert S. Norris, William M. Arkin and William Burr, 'Where They Were', *Bulletin of the Atomic Scientists*, vol. 55, no. 6, December 1999, pp. 30–1.

5   US Department of State, 'Telegram from the Embassy in Japan to the Department of State', in *Foreign Relations of the United States, 1964–68* (Washington DC: US Government Printing Office, 2006), available at https://history.state.gov/historicaldocuments/frus1964-68v29p2/d37.

6   Taka Daitoku, 'The Construction of a Virtual Nuclear State: Japan's Realistic Approach to an Emerging Nuclear Nonproliferation Regime, 1964–70', revised version of a paper presented to the Eidgenössische Technische Hochschule Zürich Center for Security Studies workshop 'Making of a Nuclear Order: Negotiating the Nuclear Non-Proliferation Treaty', Switzerland, 1 March 2014.

7   Furukawa, 'Japan's Policy and Views on Nuclear Weapon', pp. 9–10.

8   Yuri Kase, 'The Costs and Benefits of Japan's Nuclearization: An Insight into the 1968/70 Internal Report', *Nonproliferation Review*, Summer 2001.

9   Daitoku, 'The Construction of a Virtual Nuclear State'.

10   *Ibid.*

11   *Ibid.*

12   Michael J. Green and Katsuhisa Furukawa, 'Japan: New Nuclear

Realism', in Muthiah Alagappa (ed.), *The Long Shadow: Nuclear Weapons and Security in 21st Century Asia* (Stanford, CA: Stanford University Press, 2008), Chapter 12, pp. 351–2; Nobumasa Akiyama, 'The Socio-political Roots of Japan's Non-Nuclear Posture', in Benjamin Self and Jeffrey Thompson (eds), *Japan's Nuclear Option: Security, Politics and Policy in the 21st Century* (Washington DC: Henry L. Stimson Center, 2003), p. 82.

[13] Daitoku, 'The Construction of a Virtual Nuclear State'.

[14] Nobumasa Akiyama, 'Japan's Disarmament Dilemma: Between the Moral Commitment and the Security Reality', in George P. Shultz and James Goodby (eds), *The War That Must Never Be Fought: Dilemmas of Nuclear Deterrence* (Stanford, CA: Hoover Institution Press, 2015), pp. 451–2; Kurt M. Campbell and Tsuyoshi Sunohara, 'Japan: Thinking the Unthinkable', in Kurt M. Campbell, Robert J. Einhorn and Mitchell Reiss (eds), *The Nuclear Tipping Point: Why States Reconsider Their Nuclear Choices* (Washington DC: Brookings Institution Press, 2004), p. 228.

[15] Furukawa, 'Japan's Policy and Views on Nuclear Weapon', p. 20.

[16] Green and Furukawa, 'Japan', pp. 349, 353.

[17] Shamshad A. Khan, 'Japan's (Un)clear Nuclear Ambition', Institute for Defence Studies and Analysis, 11 July 2012, http://www.idsa.in/idsacomments/Japansclearnuclearambition_sakhan_110712.

[18] 'Business-as-Usual Alteration of Nuclear Law Unsettling', *Mainichi Shimbun*, 2 July 2012, available at http://www.fukushima-is-still-news.com/article-atomic-energy-basic-law-part-4-107697948.html.

[19] Llewelyn Hughes, 'Why Japan Will Not Go Nuclear (Yet)', *International Security*, vol. 31, no. 4, Spring 2007, p. 83; Mike M. Mochizuki, 'Japan Tests the Nuclear Taboo', *Nonproliferation Review*, vol. 14, no. 2, July 2007.

[20] Akiyama, 'The Socio-political Roots of Japan's Non-Nuclear Posture', p. 67.

[21] Jonathan Schell, *The Seventh Decade: The New Shape of Nuclear Danger* (Basingstoke: Palgrave Macmillan, 2007), p. 145.

[22] Hans Kristensen, 'Japan Under the US Nuclear Umbrella', The Nautilus Institute, 1999, http://oldsite.nautilus.org/archives/library/security/papers/Nuclear-Umbrella-1.html.

[23] Green and Furukawa, 'Japan', p. 350.

[24] Furukawa, 'Japan's Policy and Views on Nuclear Weapon', p. 24.

[25] Green and Furukawa, 'Japan', p. 349.

[26] Peter A. Clausen, *Nonproliferation and the National Interest* (New York: HarperCollins, 1993), pp. 87–9, cited in Motoya Kitamura, 'Japan's Plutonium Program: A Proliferation Threat?', *Nonproliferation Review*, Winter 1996.

[27] Etel Solingen, *Nuclear Logics: Contrasting Paths in East Asia and the Middle East* (Princeton, NJ: Princeton University Press, 2007), p. 58.

[28] Akiyama, 'Japan's Disarmament Dilemma', p. 437.

[29] Maria Rost Rublee, 'The Threshold States: Japan and Brazil', Chapter 5 of Tanya Ogilvie-White and David

Santoro (eds), *Slaying the Nuclear Dragon: Disarmament Dynamics in the Twenty-First Century* (Athens, GA: University of Georgia Press, 2012), p. 170.

30 Akiyama, 'Japan's Disarmament Dilemma', p. 444.

31 Author's discussions with security experts in Tokyo, November 2014.

32 Examples drawn from Kenneth J. Pyle, *Japan Rising: The Resurgence of Japanese Power and Purpose* (Cambridge, MA: The Century Foundation, 2007), pp. 366–8.

33 Sang-Moo Hwang, 'Ilbon Eui Haekmujang Chujinkwah Dongbukah Jungsae', KBS, 1 July 2012, cited in Samuels and Schoff, 'Japan's Nuclear Hedge', p. 256.

34 Etel Solingen, 'The Perils of Prediction: Japan's Once and Future Nuclear Status', in William C. Potter (ed.), *Forecasting Nuclear Proliferation in the 21st Century: A Comparative Perspective* (Stanford, CA: Stanford University Press, 2010), p. 155.

35 Author interview in Tokyo, November 2014.

36 Donald S. Zagoria, 'NCAFP Fact-finding Mission to Seoul, Taipei, Beijing and Tokyo 18 October–2 November, 2014', National Committee on American Foreign Policy, https://www.ncafp.org/ncafp/wp-content/uploads/2014/12/NCAFP-Asia-Trip-Report_November-2014.pdf.

37 Jacques E.C. Hymans, 'Veto Players, Nuclear Energy, and Nonproliferation: Domestic Institutional Barriers to a Japanese Bomb', *International Security*, vol. 36, no. 2, October 2011, p. 188. Llewelyn Hughes also argues that Japan has not implemented hedging as a 'coherent national strategy'. See Hughes, 'Why Japan Will Not Go Nuclear (Yet)', p. 69.

38 Takuya Kubo, 'Boueiryoku Seibi no Kangaekata', 20 February 1971, http://www.ioc.u-tokyo.ac.jp/~worldjpn/documents/texts/JPSC/19710220.01J.html, cited in Hajime Izumi and Katsuhisa Furukawa, 'Not Going Nuclear: Japan's Response to North Korea's Nuclear Test', *Arms Control Today*, June 2007.

39 Quoted in Daitoku, 'The Construction of a Virtual Nuclear State'.

40 Quoted in Furukawa, 'Japan's Policy and Views on Nuclear Weapon', p. 8.

41 Andrew L. Oros, 'Godzilla's Return: The New Nuclear Politics in an Insecure Japan', in Benjamin L. Self and Jeffrey W. Thompson (eds), *Japan's Nuclear Option: Security, Politics, and Policy in the 21st Century* (Washington DC: Henry L. Stimson Center, 2003), p. 51.

42 Sam Jameson, 'Official Says Japan Will Need Nuclear Arms if N. Korea Threatens', *Los Angeles Times*, 29 July 1993.

43 David Sanger, 'In Face-Saving Turn, Japan Denies Nuclear Know-How', *New York Times*, 22 June 1994.

44 Morihiro Hosokawa, 'Are U.S. Troops in Japan Needed? Reforming the Alliance', *Foreign Affairs*, vol. 77, no. 4, July–August 1998, p. 5.

45 Ariel Levite, 'Never Say Never Again: Nuclear Reversal Revisited', *International Security*, vol. 27, no. 3, Winter 2002–03, p. 71.

46 'Japanese Official Quits After Backing Nuclear Armaments', *Chicago Tribune*, 21 October 1999.

47 'Tokyo Politician Warns Beijing It Can Go Nuclear "Overnight"', Agence France-Presse, 8 April 2002.

48 Howard W. French, 'Koizumi Aide Hints at Change to No Nuclear Policy', *New York Times*, 4 June 2002, p. 10.

49 'Koizumi Denies Change in Non-Nuclear Policy amid Reports of Officials Suggesting a Switch', Associated Press, 31 May 2002, cited in Eric Talmadge, 'Controversy over Remarks on Japan Nuclear Option', *Disarmament Diplomacy*, no. 65, July–August 2002, http://www.acronym.org.uk/dd/dd65/65nr07.htm.

50 Campbell and Sunohara, 'Japan', p. 230.

51 Cited in Furukawa, 'Japan's Policy and Views on Nuclear Weapon', p. 15.

52 Chester Dawson, 'In Japan, Provocative Case for Staying Nuclear', *Wall Street Journal*, 28 October 2011; interview with Masakatsu Ota, *Shinano Mainichi Shimbun*, 25 October 2011, translated in 'Nautilus Peace and Security – 13 November', *NAPSNet Weekly Report*, 12 November 2014, http://nautilus.org/napsnet/napsnet-weekly/nautilus-peace-and-security-13-november/.

53 'Musekininna Syusho no Seissaku Minaoshiron', *Yomiuri Shimbun*, 10 August 2011; 'Tenbo Naki "datsu genpatsu" to ketsubetsu wo', Kyodo, 7 September 2011, cited in Masakatsu Ota, 'The Fukushima Nuclear Crisis and Its Political and Social Implications', in Bong Youngshik and T.J. Pempel (eds), *Japan in Crisis: What Will It Take for Japan to Rise Again?* (Seoul: Asan Institute for Policy Studies, 2013).

54 'Japan Defense Chief Morimoto Sees Nuclear Plants as Deterrent, Favors 25% Option for Energy Mix', Kyodo, 12 September 2012, available at http://www.acronym.org.uk/news/201209/japan-defense-chief-morimoto-sees-nuclear-plants-deterrent-favors-25-option-energy-mix.

55 Robert Windrem, 'Japan Has Nuclear "Bomb in the Basement", and China Isn't Happy', NBC, 11 March 2014, http://www.nbcnews.com/storyline/fukushima-anniversary/japan-has-nuclear-bomb-basement-china-isnt-happy-n48976.

56 Interview, January 2015.

57 Interview with a journalist in Tokyo, November 2014.

58 Some authors claim Japan has developed electronic triggers and other parts necessary for nuclear bombs. The source for these claims is a 1994 article in the *Sunday Times*, citing a purported UK Ministry of Defence report to the Joint Intelligence Committee (Nick Rufford, 'Japan to "Go Nuclear" in Asian Arms Race', *Sunday Times*, 30 January 1994). The newspaper has a reputation for sensationalism and does not require double sourcing for its exposés.

59 See James M. Acton, 'Wagging the Plutonium Dog: Japanese Domestic Politics and Its International Security Implications', Carnegie Endowment for International Peace, 29 September 2015, http://carnegieendowment.org/files/Plutonium_Dog_final.pdf.

60 Hughes, 'Why Japan Will Not Go Nuclear (Yet)', pp. 80–1.

61 Kitamura, 'Japan's Plutonium Program'.

62 US Energy Information Administration, 'Japan: International Energy Data and Analysis', 30 January

2015, http://www.eia.gov/beta/international/analysis.cfm?iso=JPN.

63 The Japan Atomic Energy Commission established this goal in 1956 in the first Long-Term Program for the Research, Development, and Utilization of Nuclear Energy.

64 Jeffrey W. Thompson and Benjamin L. Self, 'Nuclear Energy, Space Launch Vehicles, and Advanced Technology: Japan's Prospects for Nuclear Breakout', in Benjamin L. Self and Jeffrey W. Thompson (eds), *Japan's Nuclear Option: Security, Politics, and Policy in the 21st Century*, (Washington DC: Henry L. Stimson Center, 2003), p. 151.

65 Government of Japan, 'Strategic Energy Plan', April 2014, p. 54, http://www.enecho.meti.go.jp/en/category/others/basic_plan/pdf/4th_strategic_energy_plan.pdf.

66 Japan calls the MOX use 'pluthermal' (*plusamuru*), a Japanese combination of plutonium and thermal reactors (in contrast to fast-breeder reactors).

67 Acton, 'Wagging the Plutonium Dog'.

68 Kitamura, 'Japan's Plutonium Program'.

69 Douglas Birch, R. Jeffrey Smith and Jake Adelstein, 'Plutonium Fever Blossoms in Japan', The Center for Public Integrity, 19 May 2014, http://www.publicintegrity.org/2014/03/12/14394/plutonium-fever-blossoms-japan.

70 Victor Gilinsky, Marvin Miller and Harmon Hubbard, 'A Fresh Examination of the Proliferation Dangers of Light Water Reactors', Nonproliferation Education Center, 22 October 2004, http://npolicy.org/article.php?aid=172#_ftn_Main_22.

71 Communications with former US State Department official Fred McGoldrick, who was involved in US–Japan nuclear diplomacy at the time.

72 *Ibid*. A similar policy determination was made for India in 2010 by president George W. Bush.

73 White House, 'Fact Sheet Nonproliferation and Export Control Policy', 27 September 1993, available at http://fas.org/spp/starwars/offdocs/w930927.htm.

74 Toshihiro Okuyama, 'U.S. Alarmed about Plutonium Stockpile Growing from Rokkasho Plant', *Asahi Shimbun*, 13 April 2014, http://ajw.asahi.com/article/behind_news/politics/AJ201404130029.

75 'Uranium for 20 Nukes Repatriated from Japan in Special U.S. Operation', Kyodo, 27 December 2008.

76 Interview in Tokyo, November 2014.

77 Rublee, 'The Threshold States', p. 163.

78 Emma Chanlett-Avery and Mary Beth Nikitin, 'Japan's Nuclear Future: Policy Debate, Prospects, and U.S. Interests', Congressional Research Service, 19 February 2009, pp. 5–6, available at http://assets.opencrs.com/rpts/RL34487_20080509.pdf.

79 'Japan's Nuclear Fuel Cycle Futures: Evaluating the Nonproliferation Impact of Japan's Nuclear Fuel Cycle Decisions', summary of a workshop co-hosted by the Center for Strategic and International Studies Proliferation Prevention Program and Hitotsubashi University, 20 November 2014, http://csis.org/files/publication/141120_Report_Japan_Nuclear_Fuel_Cycle_Futures.pdf.

80 The 47.8-tonne figure is the amount of total plutonium. The amount of fissionable plutonium (Pu-239 and Pu-241) is approximately 30 tonnes, 6.3 tonnes of which is stored in Japan. Since 1994, Japan has voluntarily disclosed data about its plutonium stockpile as a confidence-building measure (but not about its HEU stocks). In reports to the IAEA in 2012 and 2013, Japan forgot to include 620kg of plutonium in MOX fuel that was stored unused at an idle power plant in Kyushu. Rectification of the mistake in 2014 generated domestic controversy, and criticism from China.

81 Interview, November 2014.

82 'MOX Imports Have Cost at Least ¥99.4bn, Much Higher than Uranium Fuel', Jiji Press, 22 February 2015.

83 Douglas Birch, 'The Projected Cost of the Government's Most Expensive Nonproliferation Effort Rises Again', Center for Public Integrity, 23 April 2015, http://www.publicintegrity. org/2015/04/23/17218/projected-cost-governments-most-expensive-nonproliferation-effort-rises-again.

84 Acton, 'Wagging the Plutonium Dog'.

85 Masafumi Takubo and Frank von Hippel, 'Ending Reprocessing in Japan: An Alternative Approach to Managing Japan's Spent Nuclear Fuel and Separated Plutonium', International Panel on Fissile Materials, November 2013, http:// fissilematerials.org/library/rr12.pdf.

86 'Japan's Nuclear Fuel Cycle Futures'.

87 Author's interview with Tatsujiro Suzuki, October 2014.

88 Fred McGoldrick, 'IAEA Custody of Japanese Plutonium Stocks: Strengthening Confidence and Transparency', Arms Control Today, September 2014.

89 Interview with Tatsujiro Suzuki, October 2014. Suzuki was vice chairman of the Japan Atomic Energy Commission at the time of the policy debate.

90 Ministry of Foreign Affairs of the People's Republic of China, 'Foreign Ministry Spokesperson Hua Chunying's Regular Press Conference on February 17, 2014', http://www.fmprc.gov.cn/mfa_eng/ xwfw_665399/s2510_665401/ 2535_665405/t1129283.shtml.

91 Interview in Tokyo, January 2015.

92 'Security Implications of the Nuclear Fuel Cycle: Report of the Monterey Eminent Persons Group', James Martin Center for Nonproliferation Studies, October 2014, http://www. nonproliferation.org/wp-content/ uploads/2014/10/141028_nuclear_ fuel_cycle_security_implications_ lewis.pdf.

93 US Department of Energy, 'Additional Information Concerning Underground Nuclear Weapon Test of Reactor-Grade Plutonium', 1994, https://www.osti.gov/opennet/ forms.jsp?formurl=document/ press/pc29.html. For a discussion of whether the 1962 test was really reactor-grade, see Gregory S. Jones, 'What Was the Pu-240 Content of the Plutonium Used in the U.S. 1962 Nuclear Test of Reactor-Grade Plutonium?', Nonproliferation Policy Education Center, 6 May 2013, http://www.npolicy.org/article. php?aid=1212&rtid=2.

94 Twenty years ago, Selig Harrison reported that the amounts were

about 40kg from Joyo and 10kg from Monju. See Selig S. Harrison, 'Unclassified Working Papers', Appendix 3 in *Japan's Nuclear Future: The Plutonium Debate and East Asian Security*, Commission to Assess the Ballistic Missile Threat to the United States, 15 July 1996, http://www.fas.org/irp/threat/missile/rumsfeld/pt2_selig.htm. I obtained updated figures from knowledgeable sources in Tokyo in October 2015.

95 Interview with Tatsujiro Suzuki, October 2014.

96 Selig Harrison, 'North Korea and the Future of East Asia Nuclear Stability', in N.S. Sisodia, V. Krishnappa and Priyanka Singh (eds), *Proliferation and Emerging Nuclear Order in the Twenty-First Century* (New Delhi: Academic Foundation, 2009), pp. 49–50.

97 Samuels and Schoff, 'Japan's Nuclear Hedge', p. 241.

98 Kazuo Takase et al., 'Successful Demonstration for Upper Stage Controlled Re-entry Experiment by H-IIB Launch Vehicle', *Mitsubishi Heavy Industries Technical Review*, vol. 48, no. 4, December 2011, http://www.mhi.co.jp/technology/review/pdf/e484/e484011.pdf.

99 Furukawa, 'Japan's Policy and Views on Nuclear Weapon', p. 20.

100 Self and Thompson, 'Nuclear Energy, Space Launch Vehicles, and Advanced Technology', p. 173; James L. Schoff, *Realigning Priorities: the U.S.–Japan Alliance and the Future of Extended Deterrence* (Cambridge, MA: Institute for Foreign Policy Analysis, 2009), p. 45.

101 Self and Thompson, 'Nuclear Energy, Space Launch Vehicles, and Advanced Technology', p. 173.

102 Dawson, 'In Japan, Provocative Case for Staying Nuclear'.

103 Schoff, 'Realigning Priorities', p. 47.

104 *Ibid.*, pp. 47–9.

105 I am indebted to James Acton for this observation.

106 Paul Levanthal, quoted in Geoff Brumfiel, 'Nuclear Proliferation Special: We Have the Technology', *Nature*, 25 November 2004, p. 432.

107 Interview with Vladimir Orlov, January 2015.

108 See Windrem, 'Japan Has Nuclear "Bomb in the Basement", and China Isn't Happy'.

109 Jeffrey Lewis, 'N Minus Six Months', Arms Control Wonk, 6 January 2007, http://lewis.armscontrolwonk.com/archive/1344/n-minus-six-months.

110 Hideo Tamura, 'Kaku Danto Shisaku ni 3nen Ijo', *Sankei Shimbun*, 25 December 2006.

111 US Deputy Director of National Intelligence, 'National Intelligence Estimate Number 4–66: The Likelihood of Further Nuclear Proliferation', 20 January 1966, National Security Archive, http://www.gwu.edu/~nsarchiv/NSAEBB/NSAEBB155/prolif-12.pdf.

112 US Director of Central Intelligence, 'National Intelligence Estimate Number 4–67: Proliferation of Missile Delivery Systems for Nuclear Weapons', National Security Archive, 26 January 1967, http://nsarchive.gwu.edu/NSAEBB/NSAEBB155/prolif-14b.pdf.

113 'A Primer on the Future Threat, the Decades Ahead: 1999–2020', quoted in Rowan Scarborough, *Rumsfeld's War: The Untold Story of America's Anti-Terrorist Commander* (Washington DC: Regnery, 2004), p. 149.

114 See Schoff, 'Realigning Priorities', p. 44.

115 Thompson and Self, 'Nuclear Energy, Space Launch Vehicles, and Advanced Technology', pp. 165–6.

116 Schoff, 'Realigning Priorities', p. 44.

117 Ibid., p. 26.

118 Zbigniew Brzezinski, The Fragile Blossom: Crisis and Change in Japan (New York: Harper and Row, 1972); John J. Mearsheimer, 'Why We Will Soon Miss the Cold War', in Andrei G. Bochkarev and Don L. Mansfield (eds), The United States and the USSR in a Changing World (Boulder, CO: Westview Press, 1992); Kenneth N. Waltz, 'The Emerging Structure of International Politics', International Security, vol. 18, no. 2, Autumn 1993, pp. 44–79.

119 CIA, 'Nuclear Weapons Production in Fourth Countries: Likelihood and Consequences', national intelligence estimate no. 100-6-57, 18 June 1957, National Security Archive, www.gwu.edu/-nsarchiv/NSAEBB/NSAEBB155/prolif-2.pdf. The national intelligence estimate said Japan would 'probably seek to develop weapons production programs within the next decade'.

120 Poll cited in Solingen, Nuclear Logics, p. 66.

121 Japan Defense Agency, 'Concerning the Problem of the Proliferation of Weapons of Mass Destruction', 1995, p. 34, http://www.ucsusa.org/assets/documents/nwgs/1995jdastudy.pdf. In common Japanese fashion, the language employed a double negative to qualify the assertion.

122 See Harrison, 'North Korea and the Future of East Asia Nuclear Stability', p. 45; Campbell and Sunohara, 'Japan', p. 231.

123 Japanese Ministry of Defense, 'Defense of Japan 2014', p. 17, http://www.mod.go.jp/e/publ/w_paper/2014.html.

124 Armed with a 1,000kg warhead, the original Nodong can travel about 900km. Tokyo is probably out of range, but not Nagoya or some parts of western Japan. A variant of the Nodong that was first displayed in 2010 might have a range of 1,600km if the warhead was reduced to 750kg. See Mark Fitzpatrick (ed.), North Korean Security Challenges: A Net Assessment (London: IISS, 2011), p. 135.

125 Matake Kamiya, 'A Disillusioned Japan Confronts North Korea', Arms Control Today, May 2003.

126 Izumi and Furukawa, 'Not Going Nuclear'.

127 Asahi public opinion poll, October 2006, http://www.tv-asahi.co.jp/hst/poll/200610/.

128 Izumi and Furukawa, 'Not Going Nuclear'.

129 Christopher W. Hughes, 'North Korea's Nuclear Weapons: Implications for the Nuclear Ambitions of Japan, South Korea, and Taiwan', Asia Policy, no. 3, January 2007, p. 87.

130 Izumi and Furukawa, 'Not Going Nuclear'.

131 See Robert Zarate, 'America's Allies and Nuclear Arms: Assessing the Geopolitics of Nonproliferation in Asia', Foreign Policy Initiative, 6 May 2014, http://www.foreignpolicyi.org/content/america%E2%80%99s-allies-and-nuclear-arms-assessing-geopolitics-nonproliferation-asia#sthash.CpJqRJwa.dpuf.

132 Interview in Tokyo, November 2014.

133 Nobumasa Akiyama, presentation at IISS workshop in Seoul, 27 October 2014.

134 Interviews in Tokyo, November 2014.

135 Interview in Washington, March 2015.

136 'Why Is China Modernizing its Nuclear Arsenal?', panel discussion at the 2015 Carnegie Nuclear Policy Conference, 24 March 2015, http://carnegieendowment.org/2015/03/24/why-is-china-modernizing/hz37.

137 Brad Roberts, 'Extended Deterrence and Strategic Stability in Northeast Asia', National Institute of Defense Studies, 9 August 2013, pp. 30–1, http://www.nids.go.jp/english/publication/visiting/pdf/01.pdf.

138 Interview with a US official, Washington, March 2015.

139 Interviews in Tokyo, January 2015.

140 Solingen, Nuclear Logics, p. 59.

141 US exports to China in 2014 totalled US$124bn, compared to US$67bn to Japan; imports from China totalled US$467bn, compared to US$134 from Japan, according to US Census Bureau figures available at https://www.census.gov/foreign-trade/balance/c5880.html.

142 Samuels and Schoff, 'Japan's Nuclear Hedge', p. 245, citing Sankei Shimbun, 22 February 2013.

143 Interview with Michael Green, October 2014. Green, who covered Asia policy for Republican presidential candidate John McCain's campaign, was one of those contacted.

144 Letter from Katsuya Okada to Hillary Clinton, 24 December 2009, unofficial translation, http://icnndngojapan.files.wordpress.com/2010/01/20091224_okada_letter_en.pdf.

145 Roberts, 'Extended Deterrence and Strategic Stability in Northeast Asia', p. 25.

146 Michito Tsuruoka, 'Why the NATO Nuclear Debate Is Relevant to Japan and Vice Versa', German Marshall Fund of the United States, 8 October 2010, http://www.gmfus.org/publications/why-nato-nuclear-debate-relevant-japan-and-vice-versa.

147 Samuels and Schoff, 'Japan's Nuclear Hedge', p. 246.

148 Discussion with Ken Jimbo, November 2014.

149 Japanese Ministry of Defense, 'National Defense Program Guidelines for FY 2014 and Beyond', 17 December 2013, http://www.mod.go.jp/j/approach/agenda/guideline/2014/pdf/20131217_e2.pdf.

150 Ministry of Foreign Affairs of Japan, 'The Guidelines for U.S.–Japan Defense Cooperation', 27 April 2015, http://www.mofa.go.jp/region/n-america/us/security/guideline2.html.

151 Discussion with Ken Jimbo, November 2014.

152 Justin McCurry and Tania Branigan, 'Obama Says US Will Defend Japan in Island Dispute with China', Guardian, 24 April 2014.

153 Bruno Tertrais, 'Drawing Red Lines Right', Washington Quarterly, Autumn 2014.

154 Shinzo Abe's remarks at Statesmen's Forum at the Center for Strategic and International Studies, Washington DC, 22 February 2013, http://csis.org/files/attachments/132202_PM_Abe_TS.pdf.

155 Robert A. Manning, 'The Future of US Extended Deterrence in Asia to 2025', Atlantic Council, October

2014, http://www.atlanticcouncil.org/publications/reports/the-future-of-us-extended-deterrence-in-asia-to-2025. Aaron L. Friedberg, *Beyond Air–Sea Battle: The Debate Over US Military Strategy in Asia* (Abingdon: Routledge for the IISS, 2014).

[156] Furukawa, 'Japan's Policy and Views on Nuclear Weapon', p. 23; interview with US official, March 2015.

[157] Zagoria, 'NCAFP Fact-finding Mission to Seoul, Taipei, Beijing and Tokyo 18 October – 2 November, 2014'.

[158] Green and Furukawa, 'Japan', pp. 358–9.

[159] Pew Research Center, 'Americans, Japanese: Mutual Respect 70 Years after the End of WWII', 7 April 2015, http://www.pewglobal.org/2015/04/07/americans-japanese-mutual-respect-70-years-after-the-end-of-wwii/.

[160] Mochizuki, 'Japan Tests the Nuclear Taboo', p. 314; Green and Furukawa, 'Japan', p. 348.

[161] Samuels and Schoff, 'Japan's Nuclear Hedge', p. 257. A related model would involve relaxing the Three Non-Nuclear Principles overtly to allow the transit of US nuclear-armed ships and aircraft.

[162] Dawson, 'In Japan, Provocative Case for Staying Nuclear'.

[163] Kamiya, 'A Disillusioned Japan Confronts North Korea', p. 67.

[164] 'Seron chosa: Abe Naikako Shiji … 71.4% Fushiji 21.8%: Kitachosen ni Taishite Atsuryoku Yori Taiwa wo Juushi 57.6%', Fuji TV, 21 April 2013, http://jin115.com/archives/51944442.html.

[165] Solingen, *Nuclear Logics*, p. 66; Samuels and Schoff, 'Japan's Nuclear Hedge', p. 251.

[166] Interview with Yukio Satoh, November 2014.

[167] Manning, 'The Future of US Extended Deterrence in Asia to 2025', p. 4.

[168] Kumao Kaneko, 'Japan Needs No Umbrella', *Bulletin of the Atomic Scientists*, vol. 52, no. 2, March–April 1996.

[169] Hymans, 'Veto Players, Nuclear Energy, and Nonproliferation', p. 180.

[170] World Bank, 'Merchandise Trade (% of GDP)', http://data.worldbank.org/indicator/TG.VAL.TOTL.GD.ZS.

[171] Izumi and Furukawa, 'Not Going Nuclear'.

[172] Reiji Yoshida, 'National Security Debate Mushrooming Since Oct 9', *Japan Times*, 25 November 2006.

[173] Brad Roberts, 'Extended Deterrence and Strategic Stability in Northeast Asia'.

[174] See David Santoro, 'Will America's Asian Allies Go Nuclear?', *National Interest*, 30 January 2014, http://nationalinterest.org/commentary/will-americas-asian-allies-go-nuclear-9794; and Zarate, 'America's Allies and Nuclear Arms'.

[175] Elbridge Colby, 'Choose Geopolitics Over Nonproliferation', *National Interest*, 28 February 2014, http://nationalinterest.org/commentary/choose-geopolitics-over-nonproliferation-9969?page=show.

[176] Quoted in Mitsuru Kurosawa, 'East Asian Regional Security and Arguments for a Nuclear Japan', paper presented at the Hiroshima Peace Institute workshop 'Prospects for East Asian Nuclear Disarmament', Hiroshima, 11–12 March 2004.

[177] David Frum, 'Mutually Assured Disruption', *New York Times*, 20 October 2006.

[178] Katsuhisa Furukawa, 'Japan's Nuclear Option', in James J. Wirtz and Peter R. Lavoy (eds), *Over the Horizon Proliferation Threats* (Stanford, CA: Stanford University Press, 2012), p. 28.

[179] Campbell and Sunohara, 'Japan', p. 246.

CHAPTER THREE

Taiwan

Like Japan and South Korea, Taiwan is often considered to be a latent nuclear power, possessing the technological basis for developing nuclear weapons. Like South Korea, Taiwan twice went down the weapons path in a post-war period of authoritarian rule and deep security anxieties. Today, the authoritarianism is gone but the reasons for anxiety remain. Taiwan faces a potential existential threat unparalleled anywhere else in the world, and its weakness relative to the Chinese mainland increases by the day. Yet non-proliferation norms are strong. A resumed nuclear weapons pursuit cannot be ruled out if the implicit US defence commitment were to wane and the positive shift in cross-Strait relations were to change dramatically. Neither condition is likely for the foreseeable future. Although a negative political shift in cross-Strait relations may be in the offing, it is not likely to change things so dramatically that it will reverse Taiwan's non-proliferation status.

History

Taiwan's secret nuclear weapons programme apparently started in late 1964, in response to the nuclear weapons test conducted by the People's Republic of China (PRC) that October. During the previous decade, Taiwan had begun to build a civilian nuclear infrastructure, thanks to participation in the US Atoms for Peace programme. Shocked by Beijing's test and angered by Washington's refusal to follow their advice to bomb the PRC nuclear facilities, Taiwan's leaders initiated a covert weapons project. Based on a US$140 million proposal by the Chung-Shan Institute of Science and Technology (CSIST), the military's main research and development centre, the code-named 'Hsin Chu Programme' was begun at the newly established Institute of Nuclear Energy Research (INER), co-located with CSIST.[1]

Taiwan did not consider its weapons programme a violation of the Non-Proliferation Treaty (NPT), which it signed in 1968. Its logic was that the NPT authorised weapons possession by the states that had exploded them prior to treaty entry into force, as Beijing had done in 1964, and since the Kuomintang government considered itself the legitimate government of all China, it was not bound by the NPT restrictions on non-nuclear weapons states.[2]

In 1969, INER purchased a Canadian 40MWt heavy-water moderated research reactor, which became operational in 1973. An ideal facility for producing weapons-grade pluto-nium, this was the same model of reactor that India used to produce plutonium for its first nuclear test in 1974. If operated at capacity, the Taiwan research reactor could have produced 10kg or more of plutonium per year, enough for up to two weapons.[3] Procuring equipment from abroad, INER also built a heavy-water production plant, a fuel-fabrication plant and a hot-cell facility for research and experiments on plutonium separation, which began operating in 1975 or 1976. INER was unable to obtain equipment to build a larger reprocessing facil-ity, although a small reprocessing plant was obtained from a

French firm. This 'Plutonium Fuel Chemistry Laboratory' was capable of producing plutonium metal.[4]

Taiwan officials had considered nuclear weapons well before the PRC test. In a 1975 speech to the Legislative Yuan, Taiwan's parliamentary body, president Chiang Ching-kuo said that research on nuclear weapons had started in 1958 (when PRC nuclear-weapons work was well under way). He added that, although he had advocated weapons development at that time, his father and president Chiang Kai-shek declined on grounds that use of such weapons would 'hurt our fellow compatriots'.[5] In 1961, during artillery battles with the mainland near Quemoy, the Taiwan military reportedly considered trying to obtain US nuclear weapons.[6] Beginning in 1958, the US deployed tactical nuclear weapons at Tainan Air Force Base on the southwest coast. They were withdrawn in 1974 in accordance with a pledge that president Richard Nixon made during, or shortly after, his 1972 visit to Beijing.[7]

Taiwan's nuclear development efforts initially took the US intelligence community by surprise. By the early 1970s, however, the US had become suspicious and taken steps to block Taiwan's efforts to procure a plutonium-reprocessing facility. In addition to intelligence assets, Washington had unusual access to Taiwan's nuclear programme because in 1972, after Taiwan's departure from the International Atomic Energy Agency (IAEA) and other UN-related bodies, the US took over custodial rights to enforce safeguards in Taiwan under a trilateral agreement. In 1974, the US Central Intelligence Agency (CIA) concluded that 'Taipei conducts its small nuclear program with a weapon option clearly in mind, and it will be in a position to fabricate a nuclear device after five years or so...'[8]

In early 1976, the IAEA learned that ten fuel rods with about 500g of plutonium metal were missing, which sparked concerns that the plutonium they contained had been extracted. In August of that year, the *Washington Post* reported that Taiwan had begun reprocessing,[9] but the story has never been confirmed. The head of the IAEA safeguards department, Rudolph Rometsch, who was a source for the article, told US officials he had only said that reprocessing could eventually take place at INER. At the time, however, some US government analysts believed that reprocessing had taken place. A US intelligence study in 1976 also claimed that nuclear scientists in Taiwan had used computers to conduct 'extensive theoretical design calculations for a first-generation nuclear device'.[10]

In September, US ambassador to the Republic of China Leonard S. Unger confronted Taiwan's leaders over the programme and was reassured that the regime would 'henceforth not engage in any activities relating to reprocessing'. When again confronted in December 1976 about reprocessing technology acquisition attempts, Chiang implied that 'overzealous officials might be conducting unauthorised activities' (in the words of a US State Department cable). At about that time, the IAEA discovered a trapdoor in the fuel pond through which fuel rods could have been diverted. Chiang's assurance proving wanting, US demands escalated, including an insistence in 1977 that Taiwan terminate all fuel cycle activities. The next summer, however, the US saw signs of a secret uranium enrichment programme.[11] Faced with US threats to cut off the supply of low-enriched uranium fuel for civilian nuclear power plants (NPPs), Taiwan in 1978 acquiesced to US demands not to develop reprocessing facilities or engage in reprocessing or enrichment. It shut down the research reactor and allowed the US to scan all of the fuel rods in its core. The plutonium fuel chemistry laboratory was also dismantled, the hot cells were converted to remove their reprocessing function, and 863g of plutonium were returned to the US.[12]

In the early 1980s, Taiwan officials discussed various kinds of nuclear cooperation with South Africa, including joint development of chemical and uranium enrichment and of small nuclear reactors. Chief of the general staff Hau Pei-tsun wrote in his diary in October 1982 that, since South Africa did not face NPT restrictions, it would be the best uranium supplier to Taiwan. Hau's diary also mentions CSIST cooperation with Israel. As published in 2000, however, Hau's diary does not indicate whether the nuclear programme still had military intentions.[13]

Some scholars surmise that Taiwan resumed its nuclear-weapons programme in the early 1980s, after the US in 1979 established formal diplomatic relations with the PRC, terminating relations with the Republic of China and the next year annulling the 1954 Mutual Defense Treaty.[14] There is no doubting that these events heightened Taiwan's sense of insecurity and distrust of the US, especially after the 1982 Sino-American communiqué, which ostensibly committed Washington to reduce its arms sales to Taiwan over time.[15] As a US diplomatic cable in January 1979 commented, it may also have been the case that Taiwan officials saw value in keeping Beijing guessing about Taiwan's nuclear capabilities. The cable mentioned how, during a defence symposium, a senior Taiwan official spoke of the need to develop nuclear weapons, saying 'we need not keep the promise [to the US] strictly and suffer'.[16] Meanwhile, US diplomats on the island continued their vigilance. Hau's diary notes that in November 1983, James Lilley, director of the American Institute in Taiwan (AIT) which replaced the embassy in 1979, expressed concerns to him about Taiwan's efforts to develop nuclear weapons. Hau denied such efforts.[17] In his diary, however, Hau expressed pride in INER's preliminary breakthrough in achieving enrichment to 0.75% by the 'chemical method', development work that violated Taiwan's agreement not to conduct uranium enrichment. Hau criticised the agreement as a 'contract to sell oneself into servitude'.[18]

In April 1986, new INER director Liu Kuang-chi told Hau that his institute could produce nuclear weapons, when ordered, within a short period of time. Having this capability was the duty of INER, he said, and would not violate the policy of not making nuclear weapons.[19] The next year, Liu made good on his claim and directed INER to quietly begin building a multiple hot-cell facility. The US discovered this move through a CIA informant, Colonel Chang Hsien-yi, who served as a deputy director at INER. In January 1988, Chang defected to the US with classified documents about the nuclear-weapons programme. The US then used this information to confront new president Lee Teng-hui, who had taken office in January 1988 after Chiang Ching-kuo's death. Lee had no choice but to agree that very month to shut down the programme, dismantling the multiple hot-cell facility. The research reactor was shut down again and sealed off with concrete, and the heavy water was sent back to the US. The reactor core was eventually removed.

How far did Taiwan get?

Several writers have cited an incorrect *Kyodo* news service story in 2000 reporting that Hau in his diary said that Taiwan had achieved a controlled nuclear test reaction.[20] What Hau's diary actually says is that, in January 1988, AIT director David Dean told him that US satellites had detected a small test explosion at the nuclear facility.[21] There is no further information in the public realm as to what this meant, but it may have been a subcritical (or cold) test, without plutonium. Taiwan had little or no fissile material with which to initiate a nuclear reaction, and had it done so the US would have been obliged to sanction Taiwan.

Hau's diary entries do not admit flatly to a government-run nuclear-weapons programme. Rather, he claims a hedging strategy: 'Maintaining the ability to, but not developing nuclear weapons is the policy of our country.'[22] He admits, however, to some work towards weapons: 'not making nuclear weapons is the set and firm policy. Naturally, a small number of scientists could not give up the result [sic] and this is not a violation of the government's policy.'[23] Like Chiang a decade earlier, he improbably claims that such work was unauthorised.

Although the research reactor produced about 85kg of high-quality plutonium in spent fuel, enough for up to 17 weapons,[24] none of this material is known to have been separated for weapons use. Taiwan officials claim no plutonium was ever separated.[25] Taiwan did have 1,075g of separated plutonium that it received from the US in 1974. As of mid-1976, it had processed 500g of this material, on claimed grounds of extracting americium.[26] Most of the plutonium and spent fuel was returned to the US in 1987–89 for storage at Savannah River. A final planned shipment of 118 spent fuel rods was blocked by a US court after local governments protested. These fuel rods, which contain about 1.2kg of plutonium, have been stabilised and are stored under containment and surveillance.[27] Claims that Taiwan has enough plutonium that could be easily processed for two to three weapons, as sources in Taiwan told a visiting British scholar in 1988, are not credible.[28]

If the Hsin Chu Programme had not been stopped, Taiwan would have been able to produce nuclear weapons within a few years. How close it came is a matter of conjecture. According to former head of the Federation of American Scientists Jeremy Stone, 'a former very high official with direct knowledge of the situation said before the defection [of Chang Hsien-yi], the scientists had done computer simulation, and while they were uncertain that everything would work, they thought that, in

1988, they were six months away from a bomb.'[29] The more common assessment, however, is that it would have taken a couple of years. In the late 1970s, State Department Taiwan desk director Burton Levin reportedly told a senior Taiwan diplomat that the US assessed that Taiwan could produce nuclear weapons in two to four years.[30] Unless Taiwan had a larger reprocessing capacity than is known from publicly available sources, it would have had to build an adequately sized facility. Reprocessing the plutonium and developing the physics package for weaponising it would have taken additional time. Although INER specialists had learned how to separate plutonium from spent fuel and turn it into metal, there is less evidence of weaponisation work.[31]

Washington's dictate to stop the programme was deeply resented by those involved, and when Chang Hsien-yi's role became public he was widely seen as a traitor for giving the US the secret evidence. Not everyone felt this way, however. In March 1988, legislator Wu Shu-chen, whose husband Chen Shui-bian became president 12 years later, praised Chang for exposing Taiwan's secret as a matter of conscience.[32]

A generation later, Taiwan's views on the matter remain mixed. Although very few people in Taiwan today advocate nuclear weapons, some of those who know the history talk about it wistfully, with expressions of regret that the US prevented Taiwan from acquiring a nuclear equaliser. Others, however, reflect that Chang in fact saved Taiwan from the unwise designs of an autocratic government, and that acquisition of nuclear weapons would have impeded the development of peaceful relations with the mainland.[33]

Nuclear latency

Taiwan is an advanced nuclear-energy economy, deriving 16.5% of its power supply from six nuclear reactors that have a total capacity of 4,900MWe. These light-water reactors were built in pairs at Chinshan, Kuosheng and Maanshan in the 1970s and 1980s. Their operating licences will expire in 2018, 2022 and 2024, respectively. In 1999, construction began on two new advanced boiling-water reactors at Lungmen, each with a 1,350MWe capacity, but numerous legal challenges and political shifts have prevented completion, as further discussed below.

Taiwan has no known enrichment or reprocessing capability. At INER, only a hot-cell laboratory and uranium conversion test plant remain in operation, the former used in connection with the stabilisation programme for the research reactor and the latter as a 'central warehouse'.[34] Without sensitive fuel-cycle facilities, Taiwan cannot produce fissile material.

The prohibition on enrichment and reprocessing that the US has insisted upon since 1978 was re-codified in 2014 when the US–Taiwan nuclear cooperation agreement was renewed. This '123 agreement' includes the so-called 'gold standard' forgoing of sensitive nuclear technologies that appeared in the US–United Arab Emirates (UAE) nuclear cooperation agreement in 2009 and which Washington has sought, so far without success, to include in such agreements with some other countries. For Taiwan, these restrictions were not an issue because of the existing bilateral understanding.[35] Taiwan's 123 agreement also included a provision similar to that of the UAE providing for advance, long-term consent for the retransfer of irradiated material to France or other agreed-upon destinations for storage and reprocessing. In February 2015, Taiwan opened its first tender for foreign reprocessing of its spent fuel[36] but soon suspended it in the face of large anti-nuclear demonstrations. To date, Taiwan's spent fuel, totalling 3,471 tonnes (including 30 tonnes of unseparated reactor-grade plutonium) as of January 2015, has been kept in cooling ponds at NPPs, but

those at Chinshan and Kuosheng are nearly full. Legal challenges and local government disapproval have delayed final
construction of urgently needed dry storage facilities.

The closure of the nuclear-weapons programme in 1988 was
final. Reflecting a normative change in line with Taiwan's tran-
sition to democracy in the early 1990s,[37] the island's nuclear
activities have remained entirely peaceful. Occasional press
reports and allegations of untoward nuclear activity since
that period have faded for lack of any solid evidence. Taiwan
leaders have occasionally spoken about maintaining a nuclear
hedge, but not in the past decade.

One incident that raised questions was an experiment in
1991 at the research reactor in which seven workers received
excess radiation doses. Atomic Energy Council (AEC) officials
refused to comment on the matter, saying the experiment was a
'government secret'. Queried about the matter by investigative
reporter Mark Hibbs, a US official hinted that the work in question involved re-irradiation of spent fuel rods to make them
less usable as a source of high-quality plutonium.[38]

Questions were also raised about research that Taiwan
undertook in the early 1990s on irradiating thorium 232-bearing
sands to produce fissile uranium 233, which it did not report
to the IAEA or to the US. After agency inspectors detected
the undeclared activity in 1994–95, the reporting failure was
quietly resolved without any publicity until Hibbs learned of it
several years later.[39] In 2005, AEC chairman Ouyang Min-shen
said the thorium research programme was unsuccessful and
was terminated.[40]

In 2004, press reports claimed that the IAEA had recently
detected unreported plutonium experiments in Taiwan. The
experiments in question, involving a few grams of plutonium
that had been imported from the US for chemical analysis,
were actually reported to the IAEA by the AEC under the

requirements of the Additional Protocol, which Taiwan signed in 1998.[41] Taiwan's was the first government with a substantial nuclear programme to accept this instrument. After extensive review of the history of the nuclear programme and Taiwan's declarations, the IAEA in 2006 was able to draw the 'broader conclusion' that all nuclear materials in Taiwan remained in peaceful activities. Because it took seven years for the IAEA thoroughly to investigate Taiwan's programme under the terms of the Additional Protocol, some critics falsely claimed that Taiwan was on an IAEA 'non-compliance list' during this period.[42] That it took seven years reflected the need for thorough review given Taiwan's history. In the case of Turkey, for example, it took ten years for the IAEA to be able to draw the broader conclusion.

In 2004, Hibbs reported concerns in Western countries about advanced metallurgical work at CSIST. After 1988, CSIST stopped its nuclear activities but continued as a research centre for Taiwan's Ministry of National Defense. According to CSIST scientists, work on thin-walled tubes made of maraging steel with a high tensile strength was related to the aerospace industry, not nuclear applications. Specifically, tubes of this general type may be used as the rotors of gas centrifuges, a uranium-enrichment technology.[43] Taiwan officials say they never had an enrichment programme, even during the 1970s and 1980s when the government pursued a plutonium-based weapons programme.[44] This assertion is contradicted in Hau's diary notes about the slight success of enrichment work. Even today, Taiwan's work in core competencies useful for nuclear weapons raises some suspicions.[45]

Since 1988, occasional statements by Taiwan officials about nuclear hedging reinforced suspicions that a nuclear option was being maintained. In July 1995, after the mainland launched six DF-15 missiles in Taiwan's direction to influence elections there, president Lee told the national assembly that 'we should re-study the question [of nuclear weapons] from a long-term point of view'.[46] Three days later Lee rescinded the statement and said that Taiwan 'has the ability to develop nuclear weapons, but will definitely not' develop them.[47] In 1998, a nuclear-hedging strategy was expressed more bluntly by Parris Chang, the pro-independence chairman of the Defense Committee of the National Assembly. He said that 'if Taiwan were to perceive no alternative guarantee to its security and a possible sell-out of Taiwan by the US ... the motivation to go nuclear would be there'.[48]

Reminding the world of its nuclear capabilities was a way to exert pressure on Washington not to abandon Taiwan and to remind Beijing that the island has options if faced with undue pressure. Gerald Segal, a British scholar who visited Taiwan in 1998, reported that, in informal briefings, officials spoke of Taiwan as a threshold nuclear state and talked in calculated terms of 'leaving options open' and 'pragmatism and ambiguity' about nuclear weapons.[49] Occasional public expressions of nuclear hedging have also been seen as a means of promoting defence spending.[50]

The nuclear-hedging strategy contributed to unsubstantiated allegations of resumed weapons work. In December 1999, a Hong Kong newspaper claimed that: 'In the wake of nuclear tests conducted by India and Pakistan in 1998, Lee ordered both the defence ministry and the academy of sciences to set up a group for guiding Taiwan's study of atomic bombs with a view to accelerating the evaluation, research and development process of nuclear weapons.'[51] In 2003, an article by a researcher at China's Academy of Military Science expanded on this claim, saying that CSIST had completed a computer-simulated nuclear explosion and that more than NT$3 billion (then US$100 million) had been spent on the nuclear-weapons programme.[52] On what basis the Chinese researcher made this claim is unclear. The year before, a nuclear scientist assigned to Taiwan's Science Council had orally recommended that the National Security Council direct a computer-assisted mathematical study of fissile material criticality. The suggestion was made in case of a future need and any such modelling would have to be in compliance with the NPT, the scientist later told this author, but nothing came of the suggestion.[53]

In August 2004, an extraordinary editorial in the *Taipei Times* called for a nuclear deterrent. Noting speculation that Taiwan would not be able to hold out for longer than two to six weeks against a missile onslaught from the mainland, the editorial argued that 'What Taiwan needs is the ability to stop Beijing from trying anything in the first place. That does not just mean the ability to inflict big losses on an attacking force, but the ability to raise the cost of attacking Taiwan far beyond China's willingness to pay. In the end this comes down to Taiwan's need for nuclear weapons. The ability to obliterate China's 10 largest cities and the Three Gorges Dam would be a powerful deterrent to China's adventurism.'[54]

Some saw the editorial as evidence of a hidden government agenda. Stone claimed to have received reliable information that national security adviser Chiou I-jen had set up a secret five-person committee to investigate nuclearisation. Other sources reportedly told Stone that INER had re-hired graduates of the 1988 nuclear-weapons programme who were again interested in reprocessing.[55] Picking up Stone's allegations, Nelson Ku, a prominent legislator, asked in the National Assembly if a government team was secretly planning the development of nuclear weapons. Premier Yu Shyi-kun responded with a denial.[56] A statement by Yu the previous month about the possible need for a retaliatory capability against the mainland had enflamed suspicions. Using the term 'balance of terror', Yu said 'if you fire 100 missiles at me, I should be able to fire at least 50 at you. If you launch an attack on … Kaohsiung [a port city], I should be able to launch a counterattack on Shanghai.'[57] Senior officials of the then-ruling Democratic Progressive Party (DPP) insisted that he was only talking about missiles, not nuclear weapons.[58] Others who were in the government at the time acknowledge that a nuclear option was sometimes discussed but say that such conversations did not lead to any action.[59]

Further controversy erupted in mid-October 2004 when the Associated Press (AP) reported that the IAEA had found evidence that Taiwan had conducted plutonium-separation experiments up until the mid-1980s. The US State Department spokesman said it was part of the agency's efforts to evaluate Taiwan's nuclear history. He cautioned that the time frame in the AP report might be inaccurate, noting the possibility that the reported experiments took place in the 1970s.[60]

President Chen Shui-bian sought to put an end to speculation by stating on 11 November 2004 that Taiwan 'will never develop these kinds of weapons and would like to urge China to openly renounce developing and using them'.[61] To dispel doubt that the second part of the sentence implied conditionality, Chiou clarified that Chen's statement was 'unilateral and irreversible'. Meanwhile, the US CIA and State Department investigated Stone's allegations and found no supporting evidence.[62] Since the 1970s, both agencies have kept a close eye on Taiwan's nuclear activities; the State Department reportedly has nearly unfettered access.[63] The IAEA also monitors Taiwan's civil nuclear programme and since 2006 has annually concluded that all nuclear materials on the island remain in peaceful use. Given that access and considering the high degree of societal transparency and press freedom that Taiwan has enjoyed since the end of the 1980s, it is highly unlikely that Taiwan has pursued a nuclear option in secret.

Non-nuclear policy

Since the turn of the century, Taiwan officials have emphasised a categorical non-nuclear policy, expressed in defence White Papers as 'five noes' – not to possess, develop, acquire, store or use nuclear weapons.[64] Many would add a sixth no: no nuclear power. In 2003, the then-ruling DPP espoused a 'nuclear-free homeland' policy. This anti-nuclear sentiment was magnified in the aftermath of Japan's Fukushima disaster in 2011. Popular opposition to all things nuclear is a reason often offered as to why Taiwan is unlikely in the foreseeable future to again go down a nuclear weapons path.[65]

After the Fukushima disaster, President Ma Ying-jeou announced that the three existing NPPs would be decommissioned on schedule and that the fourth would not be completed unless its safety could be confirmed. Ostensibly, this pledge meant a gradual phase-out of nuclear power, but Ma added conditions that decommissioning must result in no power rationing, no electricity price increases and no breaking of Taiwan's pledge to reduce carbon emissions. In April 2014, the government suspended construction of the Lungmen NPP, which by then was 97% complete at a cost of US$9.9bn, and confirmed that a national referendum should settle its fate. But under current law, the NPPs must close down by their respective expiration date, unless legislation is passed to allow extensions. In the current climate, this is unlikely.

As the DPP's presidential candidate in 2012, Tsai Ing-wen declared that nuclear power would be phased out by 2025. This remained Tsai's policy in her campaign for the January 2016 election that she won conclusively. Given the party's anti-nuclear stance, it is unlikely that the DPP government will pursue a nuclear-weapons option.

What if?

Although it is highly unlikely that Taiwan will again seek nuclear weapons, this possibility cannot be ruled out. The security condition that sparked the nuclear-weapons pursuit in 1964 and that sustained it for more than two decades – a looming potential threat from the mainland – remains the dominant risk in Taiwan's security landscape. While cross-Strait relations have improved, the military balance has steadily worsened. To the extent that Taiwan enjoys de facto protection from the US, it does not need to consider a nuclear equaliser. Two conditions thus could prompt reconsideration. If the threat perception were to become sufficiently dire and the US could not be counted upon to deter mainland China, then Taiwan would have a logical motivation to seek an autonomous A-bomb. Even then, however, the risks would probably be judged to be too great in terms of the provocation to Beijing.

Some analysts claim that if Taiwan decided to produce nuclear weapons, it would take eight to ten years[66] or longer.[67] Such estimates apparently assume a systematic development effort, similar to the past programmes of Pakistan and North Korea. Those countries had time for a measured approach since they did not face an imminent existential threat. If, on the contrary, Taiwan's security circumstances were so dire as to prompt a weaponisation decision, the government would need to embark on a crash course. Such an emergency programme that mobilised the nation's top talent and prioritised speed over safety could perhaps produce crude weapons within two years.

For a crash programme, the plutonium route would be quicker than uranium enrichment. Taiwan learned the essentials of reprocessing 40 years ago, while the enrichment programme in the 1980s never got beyond laboratory level. Although the two key scientists who led the plutonium programme are deceased, others who assisted in ancillary roles could be brought out of retirement to help jump-start a programme. While little is left of the former reprocessing-related facilities, the documentation is presumably preserved somewhere. Building a reprocessing plant might take up to one year. Weapons design work would proceed in tandem, and might be accelerated by foreign weapons designers. Weapons fabrication might then take several more months. Because Taiwan's land-attack missiles are small in diameter and thus unsuitable for crude A-bombs, the weapons would have to be designed for air drop, or possibly suicidal delivery via water.[68]

Such a crash course could not be kept secret from IAEA inspectors, the Taiwan public or outside powers. A uranium enrichment programme would be easier to hide, but probably still impossible to keep secret given the porous nature of Taiwan politics and the openness of society. Taiwan has no known uranium resources and importing the necessary uranium would itself be difficult to keep under wraps. The cost of a Manhattan Project-style weapons programme, estimated at up to US$10 bn,[69] also could not be kept confidential.

Proliferation drivers

If Taiwan were ever again to seek nuclear weapons, it would be for the same reason as before: for protection against a threat from the mainland with which the government has been at odds since the Chinese civil war of the 1940s. Today, for all intents and purposes, the dispute is not over who rules China, but rather the sovereign identity of Taiwan itself.[70] An ever-increasing majority of the island's residents feel a separate national identity, while mainland China is determined to prevent independence for the island.

The precipitating shock of 1964 was abrupt and non-conventional: Beijing's nuclear test put Taiwan's leadership in a precarious position. Any PRC effort to forcefully reunite Taiwan with the mainland would probably involve nuclear weapons only indirectly, as a threat to back up conventional force. Any actual use of nuclear weapons against Taiwan would be counterproductive to the purpose of incorporating an advanced infrastructure and population.[71] The military threat of more concern to Taiwan is the steady build-up of PRC conventional armed forces. As indicated above, if Taiwan perceived those forces as presenting an existential threat and if, at the same time, it believed it could no longer count on the protection of the US, then pursuing a nuclear option might again be attractive. Only with such a combination of these two factors, producing a profound sense of fear on the part of the population, is it conceivable that Taiwan would even seriously consider going down the nuclear path.

The cross-Strait military imbalance has steadily worsened. The PRC's military budget, after growing at a double-digit pace for 25 years, is now more than 13 times that of Taiwan, which has prioritised healthcare and social welfare over defence spending. Among other forces deployed on its side of the 160km-wide Taiwan Strait, the PRC reportedly has 1,500 short-range ballistic missiles that can target the island.[72] As a show of force in summer 1995 and March 1996, Beijing test-launched several of them into nearby waters.[73] The PRC has also conducted amphibious landing exercises on its shores opposite Taiwan. On top of the military imbalance, the mainland has an overwhelming 58 to 1 population advantage, an economic edge of 17 to 1 in GDP (in terms of purchasing power parity) and diplomatic dominance evidenced by the 174 nations with which the PRC has relations versus the 22 that still recognise Taiwan's statehood. Projecting force numbers, Taiwan's Ministry of National Defense anticipates that, by 2020, the PRC could launch a full-scale invasion that would overwhelm

Taiwanese defences.[74] Looking at the disparity, some foreign analysts conclude that Taiwan will soon face a choice between capitulation, leading to absorption by the mainland, or indigenous nuclear deterrence,[75] although this is not a conclusion shared by most observers.

In light of this imbalance, there remains a view within Taiwan military circles that Taiwan needs a powerful means of deterring the PRC and that nuclear weapons may be best suited for this role. Some retired officers speak euphemistically of the need for an 'assassin's mace' (shāshǒujiàn), meaning a weapon with which to quickly incapacitate a superior enemy. According to one retired officer who now holds an academic position, without such a weapon, Taiwan's military forces could not last beyond the first 70 hours of a concerted PRC attack.[76]

Perhaps of greater relevance than Beijing's invasion capabilities is its growing potential to complicate America's ability to come to Taiwan's defence. In March 1996, America demonstrated its naval superiority in the region by dispatching two carrier task forces to the Taiwan region. Today, US command of the sea and air around Taiwan is increasingly challenged by the PRC's emphasis on precision-strike systems and other forces intended for what the Pentagon calls an anti-access/area-denial role.[77] To counter China, the US military has been increasing its own capabilities. There remains concern, however, that the US eventually may no longer be able credibly to protect Taiwan against a strike from the mainland aimed at quickly overwhelming the island's defences.[78] The mainland also has an increasing ability to impose an air and sea blockade.

Beijing shows no sign today of readying any such options, but while it says it would only use force to obstruct independence, not to achieve unification, it does not rule out the use of force. The Anti-Secession Law that the National People's

Congress adopted in March 2005 directs the state to 'employ non-peaceful means and other necessary measures' to ensure China's territorial integrity in the event that 'the "Taiwan independence" secessionist forces' act to cause secession or close the door to unification.[79]

Since 1979, when it normalised relations with the US, Beijing's emphasis has been on peaceful unification. Abetted by growing economic interdependence and the mainland's softer approach to cross-Strait relations, tensions have been at a historic low during the past few years. Taiwan's threat perception has subsided accordingly. In 2010 President Ma Ying-jeou's Kuomintang (KMT) government negotiated an Economic Partnership Framework Agreement that contributed to making the mainland Taiwan's largest trading partner and leading choice for foreign investment. A million of Taiwan's people reside in the mainland for business. Many more benefit indirectly, including from the nearly 4m mainland tourists each year, arriving on more than 800 flights per week in summer 2015. Before 2008, there were no regularly scheduled direct flights between Taiwan and the mainland. Since then, 21 agreements have been signed between the two sides. A downside to this economic integration is the potential leverage it gives the PRC over the island, although Beijing has been careful not to use it so far. If Beijing wanted to apply pressure, economic leverage would be far more effective than military force. This is another reason why a Taiwan nuclear response to the mainland would have little logic.

Beijing's patience in waiting for its goal of unification may not be infinite. While attending the 2013 APEC summit in Bali, PRC President Xi Jinping said that political differences between the two sides 'cannot be passed on from generation to generation',[80] although Chinese officials explained that this did not mean Xi saw unification as possible within one or even two generations. Several Taiwan strategists expressed concern over the implications for Taipei in Russian president Vladimir Putin's aggression against Ukraine that year, worrying that Xi might wonder if he, too, could make a land grab without prompting a Western military response. In March 2015, Xi lashed out against independence forces in Taiwan and ominously warned that departing from the formula that has governed mainland relations under Ma could rupture the peace: 'As the old saying goes, without a solid foundation, the earth and mountain will tremble. We must adhere to the 1992 Consensus [see next paragraph], which the Chinese mainland has been regarding as the basis and precondition for conducting exchanges with authorities in Taiwan and its political parties.'[81] Two months later, Xi went a step further and said positions like 'one country on each side of the Strait' would 'undermine the fundamental interests of the nation, the country and the people, and shake the cornerstone of the development of cross-Strait relations, and there would be no possibility of peace and no possibility of development'.[82]

Xi's warnings appeared to be directed at Taiwan's voters and Tsai, who was strongly associated with Chen's position regarding the existence of two countries, one on each side of the Strait.[83] She does not accept the '1992 Consensus' under which Beijing and Taipei agreed that 'there is one China' and that each side can have its own verbal interpretation of what the one China is.[84] Although in her presidential campaign Tsai downplayed the issue of sovereignty, the DPP's formal position – and one that Tsai has vociferously advocated in the past – is that Taiwan is a sovereign independent country, not subject to the jurisdiction of the PRC. In the run-up to the January 2016 election, Tsai promoted dialogue and cooperation with the mainland, and committed not to change the 'status quo' of peace and stability or to be provocative toward Beijing. In a speech in Washington in May 2015, Tsai said the status quo included 'the existing ROC constitutional order' as well as 'the accumulated outcomes of more than 20 years of negotiations and exchanges',[85] which was an indirect reference to the 1992 Consensus. This ambiguity may suffice until she takes office in May 2016 along with a Legislative Yuan that also will be controlled by the DPP, but many observers believe thereafter that Beijing will press harder for more direct continuity with Ma's position. The absence of such continuity could bring trouble, warns Chinese foreign policy expert Bonnie Glaser.[86]

The question might thus be asked whether the DPP's return to power could conceivably set in train conditions for another nuclear push. It was under Chen Shui-bian's DPP government in 2004 that rumours raged about a secret nuclear-weapons exploration committee.[87] Chen's independence-minded policies are what prompted Beijing's National People's Congress to threaten non-peaceful means if such policies were effectuated. In theory, the DPP appears to be no less independence-minded today. In practice, however, having experienced eight years in government and eight more years preparing for another run at the presidency, the DPP is regarded as being more realistic and pragmatic. The notion that the DPP would promote both independence and a nuclear shield is dismissed in Taiwan political circles as unthinkable.[88]

As noted earlier, fear of abandonment by the US is the other factor that, in conjunction with fear of the mainland, could possibly again push Taiwan down the nuclear path as an option to replace US protection. Indeed, there could be reasons to question Washington's willingness to come to Taiwan's assistance in the future. One reason is Beijing's growing importance to the US in almost every area of economic and transnational policy, from non-proliferation to climate change. Washington insists that the China relationship will not lead to abandoning allies. Yet some American commentators have called for stopping arms sales to Taiwan in exchange for Beijing's cooperation on other issues of greater geopolitical importance.[89]

In fact, Taiwan today does not have a formal US defence guarantee. The 1979 Taiwan Relations Act (TRA), which replaced the 1954 defence treaty following the termination of diplomatic relations, is ambiguous. It declares it is the policy of the US to 'consider any effort to determine the future of Taiwan by other than peaceful means ... a threat to the peace and security of the Western Pacific area and of grave concern to the United States', to provide Taiwan with 'arms of a defensive character', and to 'maintain the capacity of the US to resist any resort to force or other forms of coercion that would jeopardize the security, or the social or economic system, of the people on Taiwan'. This falls far short of the previous commitment for military assistance under the 1954 defence treaty, even though commitments under the latter were not airtight, either.[90] US president Bill Clinton in 2004 acknowledged that the US 'had never said whether we would or wouldn't come to the defence of Taiwan if it were attacked'.[91]

When the US in 2001 designated Taiwan as the equivalent of a major non-NATO ally, it allowed Taiwan to submit military equipment requests at any time, rather than annually, but it did not otherwise change the nature of the relationship. And there has been no follow-through on a 2001 commitment to help Taiwan acquire modern submarines, of import partly because the US no longer manufactures diesel submarines and because other states that do so are unwilling to suffer Beijing's ire.[92]

Although the TRA has sometimes been interpreted to mean that the US will defend Taiwan in the case of an attack, this is not necessarily the case. To the extent that US deterrence covers Taiwan it is a de facto, not de jure, commitment, and therefore more amenable to change. There is nothing close to a Taiwan equivalent of the extended deterrence consultations that the US holds with Japan and South Korea. Taiwan is hardly even mentioned in many American analytical discussions of extended deterrence.[93] As a 2010 policy paper explained, extended deterrence is a latent issue in the Taiwan case, 'subsumed by the larger question of whether the United States would come to the island's defence at all'.[94] Think tanks find it difficult to obtain funding from US governmental and philanthropic foundations for research or Track II events on extended deterrence for Taiwan. The topic is considered too sensitive.

One last factor that could also contribute to a Taiwan nuclear push would be a breakdown in the global non-proliferation regime. If Japan or South Korea were to go nuclear in response to Chinese and North Korean threats, there would be fewer inhibitions on Taiwan doing so as well. In such a circumstance, the NPT would be a dead letter. The causation for such a domino effect would not be direct: Japanese or South Korean nuclear weapons would pose no threat to Taiwan. But since these allies would only seek nuclear weapons in the event of no longer being able to rely on US protection, there would also be a loss of credibility regarding lingering US commitments to not-quite-ally Taiwan.

Constraints

Far greater than the theoretical proliferation drivers that Taiwan faces are the practical and political constraints on any move down this path – constraints that are more powerful today than during the 1970s and 1980s. A combination of strategic and economic vulnerabilities and the near-certainty that any such effort would be revealed before it came to fruition make it highly unlikely that Taiwan would again seek nuclear weapons. Given the obvious downsides, nobody in the public realm in Taiwan today advocates nuclearisation.

During the earlier pursuit of nuclear weapons, Taiwan was ruled by an authoritarian regime, with strict press controls, a rubber-stamp legislature and swift punishment for any revelation of state secrets. Today, Taiwan is a multiparty democracy with robust freedom of speech and a raucous parliament. The budget allocation process is transparent; no public spending can avoid legislative scrutiny. As every observer of Taiwan politics is quick to point out, it would be impossible to keep a nuclear-weapons programme confidential for the period of time it would take to build them. While Taiwan would be most vulnerable when the effort was discovered, US Taiwan expert Alan Romberg notes that 'even having a complete ready-to-go weapon would not make Taiwan invulnerable. Beijing could not sit by and not respond.'[95]

The most compelling argument against Taiwan embarking on its own Manhattan Project is the vulnerability that it would invite. Beijing would probably learn of the project well before any weapons were produced, and would regard it as a *casus belli*. If war broke out and Taiwan could not count on an American intervention, which would probably be the case if Taiwan broke its non-proliferation promises, Taiwan could not hold out against the mainland for more than a month or two before munitions and oil reserves ran out. Even if an A-bomb could be produced in the shortest imaginable time period, say six months at a bare minimum, it would be too late.

Revelation of such a programme would make Taiwan immensely vulnerable. In 1998, Beijing officially asserted that the development of nuclear weapons would be an inducement for an attack on the island, putting in writing something it had unofficially made known for over a decade.[96] Although this criterion has not been repeated in subsequent policy pronouncements or White Papers, it is widely regarded as still valid and a reason why the Taiwan military would not support a nuclear-weapons programme.[97] Whether or not the mainland would use force to disallow nuclearisation, Taiwan's economic integration gives it many other ways to exert pressure.

Not only would such a move prompt Chinese hostility, it would at the same time create a negative US backlash. In light of the challenge to Washington's global non-proliferation policy and to regional peace and stability, Taiwan could not count on unconditional US support in an ensuing cross-Strait contre-temps. As international relations expert Derek Mitchell notes, 'Although Taiwan may view a nuclear option as insurance against possible future US abandonment, such a programme could make this scenario a self-fulfilling prophecy.'[98] The US arms sales and defence ties on which Taiwan relies to a unique degree would be severely jeopardised.

The US response would be scenario-dependent, of course; a conflict that was provoked by PRC aggression would not be regarded in the same way as one precipitated by Taiwan declaring independence.[99] Even if the US were to determine that Beijing was to blame in provoking Taiwan to act, at a minimum, US law would require halting nuclear energy cooperation. This move would bring Taiwan's nuclear power programme to a quick end.[100] Given America's unique status regarding nuclear safeguards in Taiwan, no other country can supply nuclear materials or equipment without US consent. In any case, all of the countries from which Taiwan buys uranium – primarily Australia and Canada – before it is enriched by the US Enrichment Corporation can be expected to be similarly disapproving. Criticism of a Taiwan nuclear weapons move would be likely to find expression in various forms of sanctions that would risk Taiwan's dependency on international trade, and exacerbate its diplomatic isolation.

Assessment

The security and economic risks underscore the political factors and physical constraints that argue against any Taiwan pursuit of nuclear weapons today. The non-proliferation norm is universally accepted in Taiwan, which accepts every non-proliferation instrument and practice in which it is eligible to participate. As in Japan, development of nuclear weapons is widely regarded as immoral, particularly by the scientific community whose talents would need to be harnessed for a strategic weapons programme. Only a deep shock to the collective psyche could change this mentality. A move by Beijing that induced such fear is not inconceivable, but it remains unlikely. Meanwhile, although the US security commitment remains ambiguous, wholesale abandonment by Washington is not likely in the foreseeable future either. Among the three democracies that are the subject of this book, Taiwan is the least likely to acquire nuclear weapons today, even though it was once the party that was the most intent on this path.

Notes

1 Derek J. Mitchell, 'Taiwan's Hsin Chu Program: Deterrence, Abandonment and Honor', in Kurt Campbell et al. (eds), *The Nuclear Tipping Point: Why States Reconsider Their Nuclear Choices* (Washington DC: Brookings Institution Press, 2004). The code name was a deception. Hsin Chu is the name of a city just south of Taipei, where National Tsing Hua University is located, although the programme was not connected with the university.

2 Monte Bullard, 'Taiwan and Nonproliferation', Nuclear Threat Initiative, May 2005, http://www.nti.org/analysis/articles/taiwan-and-nonproliferation/.

3 Technical troubles initially limited the plutonium output, which reportedly reached only about 15kg by the end of 1975 and about 30kg by 1978. See David Albright and Corey Gay, 'Taiwan: Nuclear Nightmare Averted', *Bulletin of the Atomic Scientists*, vol. 54, no. 1, January–February 1998, p. 57.

4 *Ibid*. A hot cell is a shielded concrete room equipped with remote mechanical manipulators. David Albright and Corey Gay note that, according to Taiwanese authorities, the hot cell was able to separate

only about 15g of plutonium per year. This is a small fraction of the 4–8kg that would be needed for a nuclear weapon.

5   Alan K. Chang, 'Crisis Avoided: The Past, Present and Future of Taiwan's Nuclear Weapons Program', MA thesis, Hawaii Pacific University, Autumn 2011, p. 31, http://www.hpu.edu/CHSS/History/GraduateDegree/MADMSTheses/files/alanchang.pdf.

6   *Ibid.*, p. 79. Chang cites a 2004 book published in Chinese, *Lost Secret Files of the Taiwan Military*.

7   Robert S. Norris, William M. Arkin and William Burr, 'Where They Were', *Bulletin of the Atomic Scientists*, vol. 55, no. 6, November 1999, pp. 26–35, available at http://bos.sagepub.com/content/55/6/26.full. Nuclear-armed *Matador* cruise missiles were also deployed on Taiwan from 1958 to 1962.

8   James G. Poor, 'Prospects for Further Proliferation of Nuclear Weapons', confidential memorandum from the CIA to the US Atomic Energy Commission, National Security Archive, 4 September 1974.

9   Edward Schumacher, 'Taiwan Seen Reprocessing Nuclear Fuel', *Washington Post*, 29 August 1976, p. A1.

10 Director of Central Intelligence, 'Prospects for Arms Production and Development in Republic of China', inter-agency intelligence memorandum, May 1976, pp. 8–9; cited in Jeffrey T. Richelson, *Spying on the Bomb: American Nuclear Intelligence from Nazi Germany to Iran and North Korea* (New York: W.W. Norton & Company, 2006), p. 275.

11 William Burr, 'US Opposed Taiwanese Bomb During 1970s',

National Security Archive, available at http://www2.gwu.edu/~nsarchiv/nukevault/ebb221/.

12 Albright and Gay, 'Taiwan'. According to Albright and Gay, Taiwan 'dismantled its reprocessing facilities', but it is not clear what facilities Taiwan had besides the hot cell and a small plutonium-fuel chemistry laboratory.

13 Hau Pei-tsun, *Banian Canmo Zongzhang Riji* (Taipei: Commonwealth Publishing, 2000), pp. 205, 217, 294, 327. Cited in Chang, 'Crisis Avoided'.

14 Monte Bullard and Jing-dong Yuan, 'Taiwan and Nuclear Weaponization: Incentives versus Disincentives', in William C. Potter and Gaukhar Mukhatzhanova (eds), *Forecasting Nuclear Proliferation in the 21st Century: A Comparative Perspective*, Volume 2 (Stanford, CA: Stanford University Press, 2010), p. 185.

15 Mitchell, 'Taiwan's Hsin Chu Program', p. 295.

16 Burr, 'US Opposed Taiwanese Bomb During 1970s'; US Embassy Taiwan, 'The Nuclear Option Again', cable 182 to US Department of State, 10 January 1979.

17 Hau Diary, 11 November 1983, p. 429, cited in Chang, 'Crisis Avoided'.

18 *Ibid.*, 26 January 1984, p. 469.

19 Chang, 'Crisis Avoided', pp. 88–9.

20 'Former Taiwan Military Chief Details Nuke Weapons Program', Kyodo, 5 January 2000. Jeremy Stone, who called it the last step before producing nuclear weapons, is among those who were misled by Kyodo's erroneous translation. See Jeremy J. Stone, 'Note to Blowing the Whistle', Catalytic Diplomacy,

http://catalytic-diplomacy.org/endnote.php?ch=Blowing+the+Whistle&order=17&en=59.

[21] Hau diary, 20 January 1988, p. 1,270.

[22] Ibid., 17 January 1988, p. 1,296.

[23] Ibid., 13 February 1988, p. 1,283.

[24] David Albright, Franz Berkhout and William Walker, Plutonium and Highly Enriched Uranium 1966: World Inventories, Capabilities and Policies (Oxford: SIPRI and Oxford University Press, 1997), p. 367. Research reactors are typically operated at low burn-up, which has the effect of producing plutonium with a high concentration of the PU-239 isotope, ideal for nuclear weapons.

[25] Author's interviews in Taiwan, January 2015. See also Mark Hibbs, 'Taiwan Conducted, then Halted Experiments to Produce U-233', Nucleonics Week, 23 June 2005.

[26] Albright and Gay, 'Taiwan', p. 57.

[27] Author's interviews with Taiwanese and US officials, January and March 2015. The 1.2kg calculated amount of plutonium is considerably less than the 6kg estimated by David Albright in 1997. See Albright, Berkhout and Walker, Plutonium and Highly Enriched Uranium 1966, p. 368. For confirmation of the lower amount, see Mitchell, 'Taiwan's Hsin Chu Program', pp. 301–2.

[28] Gerald Segal, 'Taiwan's Nuclear Card', Wall Street Journal, 5 August 1998.

[29] Jeremy Stone, 'Blowing the Whistle on Nuclear Plans', Catalytic Diplomacy, http://catalytic-diplomacy.org/chapter.php?order=17#en_59.

[30] Chian, Fu, Qian Fu Hui Yi Lu Juan Yi: Wai Jiao Feng Yu Dong (Taipei: Tien Hsia Yuan Chien Publishing, 2005), p. 337. Cited in Chang, 'Crisis Avoided'.

[31] Albright and Gay write, however, that 'US experts also worry that Taiwan learned a great deal about making a nuclear explosive'. See Albright and Gay, 'Taiwan', p. 60.

[32] Taiwan Legislative Yuan Meeting Note, series 23, March 1988, item 19. Cited in Chang, 'Crisis Avoided'.

[33] Conversations with scholars in Taiwan, January 2015.

[34] Briefing by INER, January 2015.

[35] Mark Hibbs, 'Taiwan and the "Gold Standard"', Arms Control Wonk, 23 July 2012, http://hibbs.armscontrolwonk.com/archive/941/taiwan-and-the-gold-standard.

[36] With the UK's reprocessing facility due to close in 2018, Russia's Mayak facility unsafeguarded and Japan's Rokkasho plant yet to start, the contract would likely go to Areva for industrial-reprocessing operations at The Hague. See 'Taipower Seeks Reprocessing Contract', Nuclear Intelligence Weekly, 20 February 2015. The new provision in the 123 agreement will prevent any repetition of the 1997 incident in which Taipower signed a contract with a North Korean trading firm to store 60,000 barrels of low-level nuclear waste at a coal mine 90km north of the border with South Korea. Protests from Seoul and Tokyo resulted in the contract being voided.

[37] Vincent Wei-Cheng Wang, 'Taiwan: Conventional Deterrence, Soft Power, and the Nuclear Option', in Muthiah Alagappa (ed.), The Long Shadow: Nuclear Weapons and Security in 21st Century Asia (Stanford, CA: Stanford University Press, 2008), p. 417.

38 Mark Hibbs, 'Seven Taiwanese Overexposed During INER Spent Fuel Movements in 1991', *Nuclear Fuel*, 19 February 2001.

39 Mark Hibbs, 'IAEA Found Undisclosed Activity on Taiwan in 1995 Inspections', *Nucleonics Week*, 15 February 2001.

40 Hibbs, 'Taiwan Conducted, Then Halted Experiments to Produce U-233'.

41 *Ibid.*

42 Chung-Kuo Shih-Pao, 'IAEA Demands Documents from Taiwan's Former Nuclear Weapons Program', 22 January 2007, cited in Bullard and Yuan, 'Taiwan and Nuclear Weaponization'.

43 Mark Hibbs, 'Centrifuge Design Proliferation Raises Questions about Taiwan Lab', *Nuclear Fuel*, 2 February 2004.

44 Mark Hibbs, 'No U enrichment Program Under "Non-nuclear" Policy, Taiwan Asserts', *Nuclear Fuel*, 24 May 2004.

45 In September 2014, a Washington-based nuclear expert, who asked to remain anonymous because he was not yet ready to draw conclusions from his research, told me that certain publications of Taiwanese researchers, some of them affiliated with CSIST, indicate proficiency with multiple technologies potentially relevant to gas centrifuges. The same expert also noted that Taiwanese metallurgy experts, in a publication on the production of thin-walled maraging-steel tubes, cited a paper co-authored by Pakistan's Abdul Qadeer Khan, of nuclear-black-market infamy.

46 Kevin Murphy, 'Taiwan Dusts Off Nuclear Threat in Its Dispute With Beijing', *New York Times*, 29 July 1995.

47 Joyce Liu, 'Taiwan Won't Make Nuclear Weapons, Says President', Reuters, 31 July 1995.

48 Quoted in Segal, 'Taiwan's Nuclear Card'.

49 *Ibid.*

50 Bullard, 'Taiwan and Nonproliferation'.

51 *Ta Kung Pao* newspaper, 29 December 1999, cited in Stone, 'Note to Blowing the Whistle'.

52 Weixing Wang, 'Taiwan hewu qizhimi' (The Mystery Surround Taiwan's Nuclear Weapon), *Shijie Zhishi* (World Knowledge), Issue 20, 2003. Cited by Chang, pp. 126–7.

53 Interview in Taipei, August 2015.

54 'Taiwan Needs Nuclear Deterrent', *Taipei Times*, 13 August 2004, http://www.taipeitimes.com/News/editorials/archives/2004/08/13/2003198573.

55 Stone, 'Blowing the Whistle on Nuclear Plans'.

56 Craig S. Smith, 'Taiwan May Have Experimented with Atomic Bomb Ingredient', *New York Times*, 14 October 2004. Nevertheless, similar questions were again raised in the National Assembly three years later by legislator Su Chi, who made the improbable claim that Taiwan had received weapons-related assistance from India and North Korea. See 'Shui Xieloule Taiwan Fazhan Hewu de Juem?', *Asia Weekly*, 15 November 2007. This time, President Chen denied the allegations in a rare question-and-answer session at the Taiwan Foreign Correspondents' Club. See Wendell Minnick, 'Taiwan President Denies Nuclear Weapons Research',

Defense News, 29 October 2007, available at http://minnickarticles.blogspot.tw/2009/09/taiwan-president-denies-nuclear-weapons.html.

57 Ko Shu-ling, 'Taiwan Premier Heralds "Balance of Terror"', *Taipei Times*, 26 September 2004, cited in Bullard Bullard, 'Taiwan and Nonproliferation'.

58 Correspondence with former DPP officials, January 2015.

59 Interview in Taipei, January 2015.

60 Paul Kerr, 'IAEA Investigating Egypt and Taiwan', *Arms Control Today*, 1 January 2005, http://www.armscontrol.org/act/2005_01-02/Egypt_Taiwanhttp://www.armscontrol.org/act/2005_01-02/Egypt_Taiwan.

61 Huang Tai-lin, 'NSC Mulls How to Make "Code of Conduct" a Reality', *Taipei Times*, 11 November 2004.

62 Interviews with former US senior officials in Washington DC, September and October 2014.

63 Mark Hibbs, 'Taiwan and the "Gold Standard"'. When Taiwan lost its membership of the UN and related bodies, in 1971, a replacement safeguards agreement signed between Taiwan, the US and the IAEA granted the US custodial rights to enforce safeguards in Taiwan in order to ensure safeguards continuity.

64 Bullard and Yuan, 'Taiwan and Nuclear Weaponization, pp. 189–90.

65 Interviews in Taipei, January and August 2015.

66 Mitchell, 'Taiwan's Hsin Chu Program', p. 302, cites Taiwanese engineers for the eight- to ten-year estimate, although he himself assigns a shorter time frame.

67 Bullard and Yuan, 'Taiwan and Nuclear Weaponization', p. 201.

68 Taiwan has no long-range missiles, but it is developing a 600km-range cruise missile called the HF-2E, the dimensions of which are unknown. Based on other systems and the size of the truck that has been used to carry the missiles, arms-control expert Jeffrey Lewis estimates the diameter to be roughly 50 60cm. This is far smaller than the 900cm weapon that China developed for its early systems, and that Khan sold to Libya. The Khan network also had designs for a more sophisticated weapon, which Lewis estimated to be about 60cm in diameter. Jeffrey Lewis, 'Red Bird Express', Arms Control Wonk, 25 January 2015, http://lewis.armscontrolwonk.com/archive/7496/red-bird-express; Jeffrey Lewis, 'Pakistani Design in Switzerland', Arms Control Wonk, 17 June 2008, http://lewis.armscontrolwonk.com/archive/1916/pakistani-design-in-switzerland .

69 Wang, 'Taiwan', p. 418.

70 Mitchell, 'Taiwan's Hsin Chu Program', pp. 193–4.

71 Wang, 'Taiwan', p. 422.

72 'PLA Aiming 1,500 Missiles at Taiwan: Defense Ministry', *Want China Times*, 1 Septemebr 2015, http://www.wantchinatimes.com/news-subclass-cnt.aspx?id=2015090 1000073&cid=1101.

73 The missile tests were meant to send a strong signal to President Lee not to depart from the one-China policy.

74 Briefing, Taiwan Ministry of National Defense, August 2015.

75 See, for example, Joachim Krause, 'Assessing the Danger of War:

Parallels and Differences between Europe in 1914 and East Asia in 2014', *International Affairs*, vol. 90, no. 6, 2014, p. 1,436.

76 Conversations in Taipei, January 2015.

77 These forces include the DF-21D 'carrier-killer' ballistic missile, an integrated air-defence system and other high-quality platforms, sensors and command-and-control and communications systems. See Elbridge Colby, 'Welcome to China and America's Nuclear Nightmare', *National Interest*, 19 December 2014.

78 Mitchell, 'Taiwan's Hsin Chu Program', p. 310.

79 Bullard, 'Taiwan and Nonproliferation'.

80 'China's Xi Says Political Solution for Taiwan Can't Wait Forever', Reuters, 6 October 2013.

81 'Xi Stresses Cross-Strait Peaceful Development', China.org.cn, 5 March 2015, http://china.org.cn/china/NPC_CPPCC_2015/2015-03/05/content_34963417.htm.

82 As translated in Alan D. Romberg, 'Squaring the Circle: Adhering to Principle, Embracing Ambiguity', China Leadership Monitor, July 2015, p. 9, http://www.hoover.org/sites/default/files/research/docs/clm47ar.pdf.

83 Bonnie Glaser and Jacqueline Vitello, 'Tough Times Ahead if the DPP Returns to Power?', PacNet, no. 41, 20 July 2015, http://csis.org/files/publication/Pac1541.pdf.

84 This differs from the 'one country, two systems', formulation that applies to Hong Kong and Macau, even though Deng Xiaoping intended it for Taiwan when he originally introduced the formula,

in the early 1980s, and it remains China's position for eventual cross-Strait reunification. Knowing that the term is politically poisonous in Taiwan, Beijing generally avoids using it, although Xi did so in September 2014 at a meeting with pro-unification Taiwanese groups. See Lawrence Chung, '"One Country, Two Systems" Right Formula for Taiwan, Xi Jinping Reiterates', *South China Morning Post*, 27 September 2014.

85 William Lowther, Tsai Vows "Consistent" Cross-strait Ties', *Taipei Times*, 5 June 2015.

86 Glaser and Vitello, 'Tough Times Ahead if the DPP Returns to Power?'

87 Two authors of a chapter on Taiwan of a 2010 text on non-proliferation claimed that members of the DPP's influential New Tide faction advocated an indigenous nuclear deterrent to protect Taiwan's independence. See Bullard and Yuan, 'Taiwan and Nuclear Weaponization', p. 192. The newspaper article they cite for this claim says nothing of the sort, however. In a week of discussions I held in Taiwan in August 2015, all interlocutors associated with the DPP claimed never to have heard anybody in the party promoting nuclear weapons.

88 Interviews in Taipei, August 2015.

89 See Bill Owens, 'America Must Start Treating China as a Friend', *Financial Times*, 17 November 2009; Charles Glaser, 'Will China's Rise Lead to War?', *Foreign Affairs*, March–April 2011; Ted Galen Carpenter, 'The Ticking Taiwan Time Bomb', *National Interest*, 20 April 2011; Paul V. Kane, 'To Save

Our Economy, Ditch Taiwan', *New York Times*, 10 November 2011.

90 'Each Party recognizes that an armed attack in the West Pacific Area directed against the territories of either of the Parties would be dangerous to its own peace and safety and declares that it would act to meet the common danger in accordance with its constitutional processes.' 'Mutual Defense Treaty between the USA and the Republic of China', Article 5, http://www.taiwandocuments.org/mutual01.htm.

91 Bill Clinton, *My Life* (London: Arrow Books, 2004), p. 208.

92 Wade Boese, 'Bush Approves Major Arms Deal to Taiwan, Defers to Aegis Sale', *Arms Control Today*, May 2001.

93 A major report by the Atlantic Council on the future of US extended deterrence in Northeast Asia is a case in point. Robert A. Manning, 'The Future of US Extended Deterrence in Asia to 2025', Atlantic Council, October 2014, http://www.atlanticcouncil.org/publications/reports/the-future-of-us-extended-deterrence-in-asia-to-2025.

94 Stephen Pifer et al., 'U.S. Nuclear and Extended Deterrence: Considerations and Challenges', Brookings Institution, May 2010, http://www.brookings.edu/~/media/research/files/papers/2010/6/nuclear-deterrence/06_nuclear_deterrence.pdf.

95 Interview in Washington DC, October 2014.

96 Mitchell, 'Taiwan's Hsin Chu Program', p. 303. Mitchell cites 'PRC Announces 3rd Reason for Use of Force', *Sing Tao Jing Pao*, 10 November 1998, p. A7. He adds that 'cross-strait observers since the 1980s have assumed, apparently through official PRC leaks, that Taiwan's development of nuclear weapons was on the mainland's list of criteria for an attack on the island. However, locating an explicit PRC statement or document from that period has been elusive.'

97 *Ibid.*

98 *Ibid.*, p. 309.

99 Manning, 'The Future of US Extended Deterrence in Asia to 2025'.

100 If, in the meantime, Taiwan followed through with decommissioning its nuclear reactors anyway, such an anti-nuclear move would have the perverse result of making Taiwan less susceptible to US non-proliferation pressure.

CONCLUSIONS

Japan, the Republic of Korea (ROK or South Korea) and Taiwan are likely to remain latent nuclear powers for the foreseeable future. Their civilian nuclear programmes and development of several dual-use technologies would enable them to produce nuclear weapons in perhaps two years – or less in Japan's case – in the unlikely event that they were to abandon their firm adherence to the Non-Proliferation Treaty (NPT). Sophisticated missile programmes in South Korea and rocket launch technologies in Japan could be adopted for warhead delivery vehicles.

The reasons for nuclear latency are varied. It is a natural consequence of seeking nuclear energy independence for reasons of energy security. It is also a subtle, and sometimes explicit, means of exerting diplomatic leverage vis-à-vis both allies and potential adversaries. Each of the three democracies in Northeast Asia faces a nuclear threat – from newly nuclear-armed North Korea in South Korea's case, from increasingly powerful mainland China in Taiwan's case, and from both for Japan. They thus have strong reasons to maintain a nuclear option. But neither nuclear latency nor nuclear hedging, which adds intent to capability, is necessarily a prelude to nuclearisation.

All three cases explored in this book have a deep nuclear history. During the Second World War, imperial Japan began projects in enriched-uranium and plutonium – the two distinct paths to an A-bomb – that quickly ran out of time and material. Driven by security fears and concern over US abandonment, both the ROK and Taiwan actively pursued nuclear weapons in the 1970s and both made a second attempt after their efforts were blocked by Washington. It may be that, at least in their second attempts, Chiang and Park sought plutonium production and reprocessing technologies for nuclear-hedging purposes. This hypothesis is hard to judge because they never got close enough to need to make a decision about actually manufacturing nuclear weapons, although the experience of most states to date is not to stop once the means are at hand.

Taipei's efforts were not extinguished until 1988, after defection to the US of a well-placed Central Intelligence Agency mole and a political change from the autocratic government of Chiang Ching-kuo. Seoul terminated its nuclear weapons pursuit in 1979 when Chun Doo-hwan, taking power in the aftermath of Park Chung-hee's assassination, needed the legitimacy of strong relations with Washington. With democracy and freedom of the press now firmly established in all three societies, it would be impossible for officials in Japan, the ROK or Taiwan to again embark secretly on nuclear-weapons programmes.

Japan's nuclear posture is unique in many ways. It is the only non-nuclear-armed state to possess large facilities for both uranium enrichment and plutonium reprocessing. It has logical, albeit debatable, civilian reasons for these dual-use technologies, but they also have been tied to an implicit, and sometimes explicit, nuclear-hedging strategy. Japan did not accept the NPT until it was assured its fuel cycle plans would not be constrained. When the US approved Japan's reprocessing programme, reluctantly by Jimmy Carter in the late 1970s and enthusiastically by Ronald Reagan in the 1980s, geopolitics trumped non-proliferation principles, while post-war Japan's clean nuclear-safeguards record was added justification. As the only country to suffer nuclear attack, Japan has a strong and enduring popular aversion to nuclear weapons. Prime Minister Shinzo Abe's intent to make Japan a 'normal' military power does not mean at all that he aspires to be nuclear-armed. After all, for the vast majority of countries, non-nuclear-armed status is normal.

Japan's so-called 'nuclear allergy' exists in tandem with reliance on US nuclear weapons for its ultimate security. The apparent contradiction of simultaneously promoting both nuclear disarmament and nuclear deterrence actually reflects basic impulses to seek peace and protection. Both postures are related to fear of China. Promoting nuclear disarmament and transparency are diplomatic tools to contain Beijing's nuclear build-up.

Although Japan's dual-use technologies put it closer to nuclear weapons status, South Korea is a more likely candidate for nuclear breakout. This is due not only to the proximity of the nuclear threat it faces from North Korea, but also to popular opinion supporting nuclear-weapons possession. In several polls over the past few years, more than 60% of the respondents voiced support for nuclear weapons. Such pro-nuclear sentiments are shallow and emotion-driven but have been further enflamed by North Korea's claimed hydrogen bomb test on 6 January 2016. A stronger educational effort by the government and civil society is needed to strengthen South Korea's non-proliferation norm.

Of the three cases, Taiwan today has the least nuclear latency even though it was once the most intent on acquiring nuclear weapons. Public suggestions for a nuclear hedge have been dormant for a decade and the island is moving away from nuclear power altogether. Yet the security condition that sparked a nuclear weapons pursuit for more than two decades from 1964 looms ever larger. Taiwan faces a potential existential threat unparalleled anywhere else in the world, and its weakness relative to the Chinese mainland increases by the day. Taiwan's Ministry of National Defense anticipates that, by 2020, the PRC could launch a full-scale invasion that would overwhelm the island's defences. Beijing shows no sign of considering any such operation and says it would only use force to obstruct independence, not to achieve unification. In the lead-up to Taiwan's January elections, President Xi Jinping issued ominous warnings, however, about a deterioration of cross-Strait relations if the winners, which, as predicted, turned out to be the independence-minded Democratic Progressive Party led by Tsai Ing-wen, do not accept the '1992 Consensus' that there is but one China. Taiwan's security future is thus clouded.

However strong the motivations for the three democracies to maintain nuclear latency, the reasons for not fulfilling the nuclear option are far stronger in each case. Going nuclear would provoke antagonists and other neighbours, jeopardise security and trade, risk defence ties, undermine international order and disparage the nation's name.

In South Korea's case, for example, pursuing nuclear weapons would result in the cut-off of foreign-supplied uranium fuel for the nation's 23 power reactors under the terms of bilateral nuclear cooperation agreements. Seoul's high hopes for becoming a leading nuclear technology exporter would wither. The idea that acquiring nuclear weapons of its own would pressure Pyongyang to negotiate the end of its own nuclear programme would be a desperate gamble. Denuclearising North Korea would become ever more distant and the peninsula would be left with an enduring nuclear stand-off. It is also hard to see circumstances under which US tactical nuclear weapons could be returned to South Korea, as suggested by some Seoul-based pundits. US officials, both civilian and military, are thoroughly opposed to the idea, for very good reasons. The stationing cost would be high and the weapons would be at risk. Meanwhile, tactical nuclear weapons in South Korea would have no military use that could not be served by either conventional weapons or US strategic nuclear weapons launched from submarines, missiles or long-range bombers.

Non-proliferation role of extended deterrence

Non-proliferation in Northeast Asia depends foremost on the credibility of US deterrence. There is no reason for any of the three actors to entertain the risks associated with indigenous nuclear weapons as long as they can rely on the US for ultimate security. Even Taiwan, which does not enjoy an explicit US alliance relationship, can count on de facto US protection. To state the converse, a failure of the US to ensure effective deterrence would be the strongest stimulant to a proliferation cascade in Northeast Asia. Japan, for example, worries about China's recent nuclear force modernisation. There is equal if not greater concern about China's growing conventional anti-access/area-denial capabilities and whether they might someday preclude America's ability to come to Japan's defence. Combined with China–US mutual vulnerability at the strategic level, a perceived superiority of China's conventional capabilities conceivably could cause Japan to consider a nuclear dimension of its own. In Taiwan, notwithstanding the trend against all forms of nuclear technology, resumed tensions with the mainland that appear on the horizon mean that nuclear-hedging options cannot be ruled out, especially if the US were to become isolationist or its perceived commitment to defend

Taiwan were to weaken. In the Korean Peninsula, a loss of credibility of the US extended deterrence could make the nuclear imbalance between North and South intolerable to Seoul.

US retreat from Northeast Asia is unlikely. Successive US administrations have given high priority to extended deterrence, in both word and deed. Obama's 'pivot to East Asia' or rebalancing policy extended a similar posture of the George W. Bush administration. The Pentagon is developing countermeasures to China's capabilities, and Obama has reassured Japan that the Security Treaty commitment applies to the Senkaku/Diaoyu islands, the Japanese-administered territory that is most susceptible to Chinese 'grey-zone' provocations. The emphasis in the 2015 US–Japan defence guidelines on 'seamless' bilateral responses provided additional reassurances. The unsurpassed current strength of the US alliances with both Japan and the ROK lends confidence to a prediction that neither country will go nuclear in the foreseeable future.

The credibility of deterrence depends as much on perceptions as on the reality of maintaining defence assets in the region and the will to use them, as well as strategic assets elsewhere. One little-noticed but important aspect of Obama's East Asia policy has been the establishment of regular deterrence dialogues with both Japan and South Korea. The biannual Extended Deterrence Dialogue with Japan and the Extended Deterrence Policy Committee with South Korea give the East Asian allies a sense of inclusion in nuclear planning that was hitherto reserved to NATO. The dialogues are a useful means of addressing Japanese concerns about accepting strategic stability with China and for coordinating with South Korea over nuclear signalling to Pyongyang. They are a tangible and visible way to underscore the promise of extended deterrence with none of the downsides of the unlikely alternative of redeploying US tactical nuclear weapons in the region. But the discussions are not limited to nuclear deterrence. The full spectrum of the deterrence equation includes ballistic missile defence, cyber capabilities and conventional responses. The durability of these dialogues is important. Whoever succeeds Obama as president in 2017 would be well advised to keep the senior-level consultative mechanisms in place.

Balancing nuclear and non-nuclear aspects of deterrence will be a continual challenge. Obama's impulse to reduce the salience of nuclear weapons in US national security strategy has been tempered by the concerns of Asian allies not to signal lack of resolve in countering nuclear threats. In revising the Nuclear Posture Review in 2010, the Obama administration took Japanese and ROK concerns into account in deciding against declaring that the sole purpose of nuclear weapons is to deter use of nuclear weapons by others. Those consultations played an important role in sustaining confidence in the credibility of US extended deterrence. Unless its allies were to change their stance and come out for a no-first-use policy, the US is unlikely to adopt such a nuclear policy.

The reality, however, is that nuclear use is neither entirely credible nor necessary for deterring most of the threats that America and its partners may face in Northeast Asia. Modernised conventional capabilities can be better calibrated to counter the entire range of potential provocations, with none of the taboos that have become attached to nuclear weapons. Nuclear deterrence remains vital, of course, particularly to deter nuclear threats. But other forms of deterrence will come into play earlier in nearly every scenario. Washington thus has sought assiduously to address Japanese and ROK anxieties about low-level provocations by sustaining capabilities across the spectrum. US non-military engagement in East Asia, including free trade pacts and political ties, further enhances the credibility of US deterrence. Attributing special significance to a 'nuclear umbrella' helps to reassure allies, but it is a misnomer. Atomic retaliation is but one thread of what must be an interwoven fabric of the deterrence posture.

Over the years, under both Democratic and Republican administrations, the US has consistently worked diligently to keep its allies non-nuclear, employing both threats and inducements. Non-proliferation can be expected to remain a priority under any future US president. It will be important for policymakers and opinion-shapers not to signal otherwise. When vice-president Dick Cheney and other influential Washington figures warned in the early part of the century that Pyongyang's nuclear pursuit could prompt Japan's nuclearisation, it gave A-bomb proponents in Japan a false impression that the US would welcome this development. Playing the 'Japan card' in this fashion would risk becoming a self-fulfilling prophecy by implying tacit approval.

While extended-deterrence guarantees can be expected to keep nuclear dominoes at bay in Northeast Asia, there is less reason for equanimity concerning nuclear-hedging strategies. An expansion of fissile material production capabilities is the most pressing proliferation challenge of the twenty-first century. Although the Middle East currently commands the most attention in this regard, as Saudi Arabia and perhaps other neighbours consider seeking to match the uranium enrichment capability that has now been legitimised for Iran, Northeast Asia is an equally pertinent place to watch.

In the wake of the Fukushima nuclear disaster in 2011, when many Japanese questioned the merits of nuclear power, former defence minister Shigeru Ishiba advocated keeping the nuclear fuel cycle in order to maintain 'technical deterrence'. The accumulation of 47 tonnes of currently unusable plutonium is due largely to bureaucratic inertia and poor bets on technology advances, not because Japan thought it might need to be the first nation to use reactor-grade plutonium for weapons. But even though the main reason was for energy security, the reprocessing technology as well as uranium enrichment were developed partly with a hedging strategy in mind.

In turn, Japan's possession of sensitive fuel-cycle technologies fanned South Korean interest in plutonium reprocessing of its own. An updated nuclear cooperation agreement with the US in 2015 put off for six more years Seoul's quest for a form of this technology, called pyroprocessing, which is only slightly less of a proliferation concern. Japan's upcoming decision to start reprocessing at Rokkasho will fan popular resentment over unequal treatment. Japan could make a great contribution to global non-proliferation by abandoning reprocessing.

Two final considerations are warranted concerning the Korean Peninsula. Firstly, North Korea cannot be accepted as a nuclear-armed state. Its international interlocutors must instead continue always to insist on denuclearisation and to mean it. Appearing to acquiesce in de facto nuclear status for the North would fan impulses in the ROK to seek a nuclear equaliser. While insisting on rollback, however, efforts must simultaneously be made to cap North Korea's nuclear and missile programmes, through a combination of the kind of sanctions, engagement and deterrence policies that served to stem Iran's nuclear capabilities. Restraining North Korea will also reduce the incentive for South Korea and Japan to seek nuclear weapons.

Secondly, in the event of the wild-card scenario of North Korean collapse, it will be imperative to ensure that all of Pyongyang's nuclear-weapons infrastructure is removed or destroyed. The nuclear weapons scientists must then be re-employed in civilian capacities, as was done with former Soviet weapons scientists. Any unified Korean state that emerges should leave no doubt of its non-nuclear posture.

Firm adherence to the NPT by a unified Korea combined with US partnership would obviate what otherwise could be the strongest motivation for Japan to increase its nuclear hedge.

INDEX

Adelphi books are published eight times a year by Routledge Journals, an imprint of Taylor & Francis, 4 Park Square, Milton Park, Abingdon, Oxfordshire OX14 4RN, UK.

A subscription to the institution print edition, ISSN 1944-5571, includes free access for any number of concurrent users across a local area network to the online edition, ISSN 1944-558X. Taylor & Francis has a flexible approach to subscriptions enabling us to match individual libraries' requirements. This journal is available via a traditional institutional subscription (either print with free online access, or online-only at a discount) or as part of the Strategic, Defence and Security Studies subject package or Strategic, Defence and Security Studies full text package. For more information on our sales packages please visit www.tandfonline.com/librarians_pricinginfo_journals.

2016 Annual Adelphi Subscription Rates			
Institution	£651	$1,144 USD	€965
Individual	£230	$393 USD	€314
Online only	£570	$1,001 USD	€844

Dollar rates apply to subscribers outside Europe. Euro rates apply to all subscribers in Europe except the UK and the Republic of Ireland where the pound sterling price applies. All subscriptions are payable in advance and all rates include postage. Journals are sent by air to the USA, Canada, Mexico, India, Japan and Australasia. Subscriptions are entered on an annual basis, i.e. January to December. Payment may be made by sterling cheque, dollar cheque, international money order, National Giro, or credit card (Amex, Visa, Mastercard).

For a complete and up-to-date guide to Taylor & Francis journals and books publishing programmes, and details of advertising in our journals, visit our website: http://www.tandfonline.com.

Ordering information:
USA/Canada: Taylor & Francis Inc., Journals Department, 325 Chestnut Street, 8th Floor, Philadelphia, PA 19106, USA. **UK/Europe/Rest of World:** Routledge Journals, T&F Customer Services, T&F Informa UK Ltd., Sheepen Place, Colchester, Essex, CO3 3LP, UK.

Advertising enquiries to:
USA/Canada: The Advertising Manager, Taylor & Francis Inc., 325 Chestnut Street, 8th Floor, Philadelphia, PA 19106, USA. Tel: +1 (800) 354 1420. Fax: +1 (215) 625 2940. **UK/Europe/Rest of World**: The Advertising Manager, Routledge Journals, Taylor & Francis, 4 Park Square, Milton Park, Abingdon, Oxfordshire OX14 4RN, UK. Tel: +44 (0) 20 7017 6000. Fax: +44 (0) 20 7017 6336.

The print edition of this journal is printed on ANSI conforming acid-free paper by Bell & Bain, Glasgow, UK.